Professional English in Use

Marketing

Cate Farrall
Marianne Lindsley

CAMBRIDGE
UNIVERSITY PRESS

CAMBRIDGE UNIVERSITY PRESS

Cambridge, New York, Melbourne, Madrid, Cape Town, Singapore, São Paulo, Delhi

Cambridge University Press
The Edinburgh Building, Cambridge CB2 8RU, UK

www.cambridge.org
Information on this title: www.cambridge.org/9780521702690

© Cambridge University Press 2008

This publication is in copyright. Subject to statutory exception
and to the provisions of relevant collective licensing agreements,
no reproduction of any part may take place without the written
permission of Cambridge University Press.

First published 2008
Reprinted 2009

Produced by Kamae Design, Oxford

Printed in Dubai by Oriental Press

A catalogue record for this publication is available from the British Library

ISBN 978-0-521-70269-0 Edition with answers

Cambridge University Press has no responsibility for the persistence or
accuracy of URLs for external or third-party internet websites referred to in
this publication, and does not guarantee that any content on such websites is,
or will remain, accurate or appropriate. Information regarding prices, travel
timetables and other factual information given in this work are correct at
the time of first printing but Cambridge University Press does not guarantee
the accuracy of such information thereafter.

Contents

Introduction

Who is this book for?

Professional English in Use Marketing presents the vocabulary and expressions required to speak about marketing and related fields. It is designed to help those who work in marketing and need to use English. It will also help marketing students preparing for their first contacts with English speakers or studying for exams in English. The level of the book is intermediate to upper-intermediate.

This book assumes you know, or are in the process of learning from your marketing course, common marketing and communication concepts (such as *the marketing mix* and *targeting*). Our focus is on the words that are often used by professionals when talking and writing about marketing (such as *core target* and *focus groups*) and on English words which are given a special meaning in marketing (such as *buzz* and *loyalty*). Every unit uses authentic sources, including marketing forums, company websites, articles from the trade press, marketing blogs, marketing presentations, and case studies.

You can use the book on your own for self-study, or with a teacher in the classroom, one-to-one or in groups.

How is the book organized?

The book has 50 two-page thematic units. The units are divided into ten sections which cover topics such as **Product, Price** and **Place**. The first section, **Marketing basics**, introduces essential marketing vocabulary and concepts which you will need to tackle the more specialized units later in the book.

The left-hand page of each unit explains new words and expressions and shows how the vocabulary is used in real contexts. The right-hand page allows you to check and develop your understanding of the new language and how it is used, through a series of exercises. There is cross-referencing between units to help you develop your vocabulary.

There are twelve **appendices**, covering examples of confusing words, preparing a marketing plan, talking about numbers, describing brand values, market segments, indirect distribution methods, advertising techniques, TV and radio dayparts and programmes, types of out-of-home advertising, types of magazine, a newspaper rate card, and mailshot items.

There is an **answer key** at the back of the book. Most of the exercises have questions with only one correct answer. But some of the exercises, including the **Over to you** activities at the end of each unit (see opposite), are designed for writing and / or discussion.

There is also an **index**, which lists all the new words and expressions presented in the book and gives the unit numbers where they appear. It also indicates how the terms are pronounced.

The left-hand page

This page presents the key vocabulary in bold typeface for each theme or skills area. The language is introduced in a series of short texts, dialogues, diagrams and tables. Many vocabulary items are illustrated. Each unit has sections indicated by a letter – usually A, B and C – and a clear title.

In addition to vocabulary explanations, this page includes information about typical collocations (word combinations) and register (formal and informal language).

There are also **notes** on language points, for example where a particular grammatical form is associated with a word, or where the same word may have different uses.

The right-hand page

The exercises on the right-hand page allow you to check your understanding and give you practice in using the words and expressions presented on the left-hand page. There are a variety of exercises including crosswords, short texts, gap fills, matching exercises, and tables to complete.

'Over to you' sections

An important feature of *Professional English in Use Marketing* is the **Over to you** section at the end of each unit. This is your opportunity to put into practice the words and expressions in the unit by relating it to your professional situation, studies or opinions.

How to use the book for self-study

We suggest all learners start with the **Marketing basics** section. Learners can then work systematically through the book or pick topics that interest them from the **contents** page.

Read through the texts on the left-hand page. If you meet words which you consider important and which are not explained in the text, look at the index to see if they are explained in another unit. Do the exercises on the right-hand page and check your answers in the key. If you find you have made mistakes, go back to the left-hand page and read through the texts again. Do the **Over to You** section and make sure that you use as many new words as possible. You should present your ideas out loud and ideally record yourself. The index gives help with pronunciation.

How to use the book in a classroom

Teachers can use this book as a framework for an 'English for Marketing' course or to supplement more general course books. The illustrations can often be used as a warm-up activity or as a talking point during the class. Sometimes, the left-hand page may be used as the basis for a presentation, either by the teacher or the learners. Learners can do the exercises individually or in small groups. They can compare answers in the groups or as a whole class feedback session. In the classroom, the **Over to you** sections can be used as a starting point for role plays, discussions and presentation activities, or adapted to out-of-class projects.

We hope you enjoy using this book.

Professional English in Use

Professional English in Use Marketing is part of a new series of **Professional English in Use** titles from Cambridge University Press. These books offer vocabulary reference and practice for specialist areas of professional English. Have you seen some of the other titles available in the series?

1 The marketing mix 1

A The Ps

The **marketing mix** is the combination of techniques used to **market a brand**. The techniques are often called **the Ps**. Originally there were four Ps:

- **Product** (or service): what you sell, and the variety or **range** of products you sell. This includes the **quality** (how good it is), **branding** (see Units 16–18), and **reputation** (the opinion the consumers have) of the product. For a service, **support** for the client after the purchase is important. For example, travel insurance is often sold with access to a telephone helpline in case of emergency.
- **Price:** how much the product or service costs.
- **Place:** where you sell the product or service. This means the **location** of your shop, or **outlet,** or the **accessibility** of your service – how easy it is to access.
- **Promotion:** how you tell consumers about the product or service. The **promotional mix** is a blend of the **promotional tools** used to communicate about the product or service – for example, TV **advertising**.

Today some marketers talk about an additional four Ps:

- **People:** how your **staff** (or employees), are different from those in a competitor's organization, and how your clients are different from your competitor's clients.
- **Physical presence:** how your shop or website looks.
- **Process:** how your product is built and delivered, or how your service is sold, delivered and accessed.
- **Physical evidence:** how your service becomes **tangible**. For example, tickets, policies and brochures create something the customers can touch and hold.

B Marketing a new product

A small educational games company is launching a new game to teach English vocabulary to beginner learners. The marketing manager, Dominic Dangerfield, is making a presentation using PowerPoint slides.

> **The Turnover Game**
>
> PRODUCT:
> - Innovative way to learn new vocabulary
> - **Launch:** how we are planning to introduce the product onto the market
>
> PLACE
> - **Distribution:** high street retailers and mail order via website and catalogues
> - **Delivery:** five days by mail order or straightaway in shops
>
> PROMOTION
> - **Advertising:** in children's magazines
> - **Direct marketing:** insert catalogue in *Parent* magazine
>
> PEOPLE
> - **Customers:** educated, city-dwellers with pre-teen children, school teachers
> - **Competitors:** they have a larger **sales force** to sell their products
>
> PRICE
> - **Premium pricing:** 20% above market average for a CD-ROM
> - **Special deals:** 15% discount for schools

Note: For more information on sales promotion, see Unit 41.

1.1 A marketing manager is talking about the marketing mix for a brand of cleaning products. Choose the correct words from the brackets to complete the text, and then match each speech bubble with one of the Ps. Look at A opposite to help you.

1
Our (staff / reputation / competitors) are highly motivated. We really believe in our brand. For example, our (consumers / employees / customers) are always trying to improve what we do.

2
Our (tools / range / support) includes detergent, toilet cleaner and sponges.

3
We use a lot of (advertising / presence / promotional), usually in women's magazines.

4
You can find the brand in supermarkets and local shops. The (tangible / accessibility / process) of our (staff / mix / outlets) is important. We need to be in a lot of (locations / supports / distributions) so that we are easy to find.

5
We are more (accessibility / reputation / expensive) than our (competitors / staff / sales) but we offer good credit terms and we sometimes run special (deals / processes / support).

1.2 Complete the text using words from the box. Look at A opposite to help you.

advertising	mix	price	products	promotional

Marie Curie Cancer Care is reviewing its marketing strategy in an attempt to attract a wider audience. It will stop using (1) .... techniques, such as mailings and events. Television (2) .... and face-to-face marketing are both being tested in a bid to supplement the charity's typical over-60s donor base with younger supporters. If tests prove successful, they will become part of Marie Curie's marketing (3) ....

In addition, Marie Curie Cancer Care is expanding its online shop. Stylish handbags at a (4) .... of £10 are attractive to younger customers. Marie Curie Cancer Care says it is responding to customers' needs and wants by selling elegant fashionwear (5) ....

1.3 Do the following words and expressions refer to product, price, place, promotion, or people? Look at A and B opposite to help you.

accessibility	customers	discounts	location	sales force
branding	delivery	distribution	quality	special deals
competitors	direct marketing	launch	reputation	support

Product	Price	Place	Promotion	People

Over to you

Think about an expensive brand and a less expensive alternative – for example, Bang & Olufsen compared to Sony. What are the differences in the marketing mix for the two brands?

2 The marketing mix 2

A The four Cs, As and Os

Some marketers have supplemented the four Ps (see Unit 1) with new ways of thinking about marketing. The Ps, **Cs**, **As** and **Os** can be combined when looking at the marketing mix.

4Ps	4Cs	4As	4Os
Product	**Customer needs** What does the customer need to **solve a problem**? For example, people don't have time to cook – we offer the solution of frozen dinners. The company must **identify customer needs** so that products that **meet these needs** can be developed (see Units 10–11).	**Acceptability** How **acceptable** is the product, and do people approve of the product? Is it **socially acceptable** – **fashionable** and **attractive**? Does the product respect the laws of the country – is it **legally acceptable**?	**Objects** What do you sell? How is it **manufactured**, or made? Is it a **high quality** (or excellent) product, or is it **bottom end**?
Price	**Cost to user** Does the customer **perceive the cost** of the product as fair, or is it too expensive?	**Affordability** Does the customer have enough money to buy the product – can he / she **afford** the product?	**Objectives** **Revenue objectives** concern the income you want to generate. **Price objectives** concern the price you want to sell at.
Place	**Convenience** How **convenient** is it to find your product? Is it easy, or does the customer have to **make an effort**?	**Accessibility** Is the product **easy to access**? Is the product **accessible** for people with disabilities?	**Organization** How should you **organize** the sale and distribution of your product? Which **distribution methods** (see Unit 26) will work best?
Promotion	**Communication** How should you **communicate** with your customers?	**Awareness** How many people know about, or are **aware of**, the product? Is awareness **high**?	**Operations** Which kind of **promotional operations**, such as direct mail, will work best for the product? (See Units 32–43)

Note: **Customer** or **client**? See Appendix I on page 108.

B AIDA

AIDA is an acronym which represents the steps a marketer takes in order to persuade customers to buy a product or service.

Attention	Marketing must first **attract** the customers' **attention to** the product. Customers **become aware of** a product and know it is available.
Interest	Then, marketing must **create an interest in** the product. Customers will **develop an interest in** the product.
Desire	Next, marketing must **develop a desire** to own or have the product so that customers **actively want** the product.
Action	Finally, marketing must **prompt action** to purchase, so that customers **take steps** to buy the product – for example, by going to the shop or ordering it online.

2.1 Put the words and expressions from the box into the correct columns. Look at A opposite to help you.

acceptability	awareness	cost to user	objects
accessibility	communication	customer needs	operations
affordability	convenience	objectives	organization

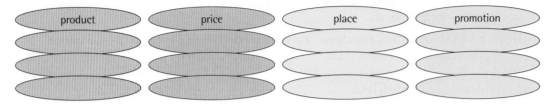

| product | price | place | promotion |

2.2 Complete the article about a supermarket in-store event using words from the box. Look at A opposite to help you.

| awareness | customers | identified | meet | promotional |

This week, Tesco launches its biggest ever 'Health Event' – illustrating its commitment to helping (1) .... lead a healthy and active lifestyle. The supermarket has (2) .... health as an important customer concern and is working to (3) .... the needs of its customers.

Hundreds of (4) .... operations for healthy products will run all over the store, from fresh produce through to grocery and healthcare lines. Tesco hopes that (5) .... of its initiative will be high.

2.3 Replace the underlined words and expressions with alternative words and expressions from the box. Look at A opposite to help you.

| afford | high quality | revenue objectives |
| convenient | price | socially acceptable |

1 Mobile phones are <u>fashionable and attractive</u> to the youth market.
2 We have a reputation for providing <u>good standard</u> mobile phones.
3 The <u>cost to user</u> of mobile phones is kept down because they are subsidized by the network providers.
4 This means more people can <u>have the money to buy</u> the product.
5 More and more, customers buy mobile phones online because it is more <u>accessible</u>.
6 <u>Expected earnings</u> from 3G phones were not met when the products were first launched.

2.4 Put the words in each sentence in the correct order. Look at B opposite to help you.

1 attention attract must product the to We.
2 aware become of People brand the will.
3 an create in interest need product the to We.
4 an customers develop in interest product the to want We.
5 a desire develop must our own product to We.
6 People steps take it to try will.
7 action buy must prompt it to We.

Over to you

Think about the most recent product you bought. Describe the marketing mix using the 4Cs, the 4As or the 4Os.

3 SWOT analysis

A SWOT analysis

Before entering the marketplace it is essential to **carry out** a **SWOT analysis**. This **identifies** the **strengths** and **weaknesses** of a product, service or company, and the **opportunities** and **threats** facing it. Strengths and weaknesses refer to the product itself and are considered as **internal factors**. The **external factors**, referring to the marketplace, are opportunities and threats.

This is a SWOT analysis of PetraServe, a company which runs motorway service stations.

STRENGTHS	WEAKNESSES
Superior distribution network – we have one of the best.	Undifferentiated offer in terms of basic product – petrol is the same whatever the brand.
We are the specialist in long-distance petrol needs for lorry and truck drivers – we have experience, knowledge and skill.	Lack of new products – we need more.
Consumers see us as a quality brand.	Ineffective leverage of specialist image – we don't use our specialist image well.
Innovative loyalty programme that's unique in the market.	Inferior communication – we could communicate better.
We are a profitable company – we're making money.	Damaged reputation for petrol and fossil fuels – they have a bad image.
Highly recognizable brand. A global brand.	Consumer loyalty is weak.

OPPORTUNITIES	THREATS
Developing market for service station shop (confectionery, car maintenance products, etc.).	Our main competitor is strong.
Gap in the market: hybrid cars and electric cars will need fuel.	Price war in the fuel market is becoming more threatening – all our competitors are cutting prices.
Huge potential for growth – there is a lot of room to expand into new markets.	Emerging trend towards hybrid cars and electric cars.
	Consumer fears about environment and pollution.

B SWOT and marketing strategy

Pat Albright is the senior marketing manager for PetraServe. She's presenting her marketing strategy to the board. The strategy was shaped by the SWOT analysis above.

'We need to **exploit** our **strengths** by making the most of our distribution network and loyalty programme. If we can also **build on strengths** such as our brand image and current profitability, then it'll be easier to **address**, or deal with, **weaknesses** such as the lack of new products. We need to **anticipate the threat** of new hybrid cars and **seize** the new **opportunities** this will bring in terms of providing service points for these cars. The potential price war in the fuel market **poses a serious threat** and we will need to **minimize** the **weaknesses** this may create. Our sector **is** also **under threat from** the trend towards greater consumer concerns about the environment, but I believe we can **create an opportunity** by **strengthening** our **communication** and **informing consumers** about what we're doing to preserve the environment.'

3.1 The extracts below are from a SWOT analysis. Do they describe strengths, weaknesses, opportunities or threats? Look at A opposite to help you.

1
> Competition is growing in this market, which could lead to a price war. There are now a lot of sites that offer the same service and product categories as Amazon. Amazon is a global brand but in some local markets the main competitor could be stronger and preferred by consumers.

2
> Amazon has added a lot of new categories, but this may damage the brand. For example, offering automobiles may be confusing for customers. Due to increased competition, the offer is undifferentiated.

3
> In 2004 Amazon moved into the Chinese market. There is huge potential here. In 2005 Amazon launched a new loyalty programme, AmazonPrime, which should maximize purchases from the existing client base.

4
> Amazon is a global brand, operating in over ten countries. It was one of the first online retailers and today it has an enormous customer base. It has built on early successes with books, and now has product categories that include jewellery, toys and games, food and more. It has an innovative Customer Relationship Management programme.

3.2 Complete the table with words from A and B opposite and related forms. Then complete the sentences below using words from the table.

Verb	Noun	Adjective
		opportune
strengthen		
threaten		
weaken		

1 Currently, the company is under .... from its main competitors.
2 In order to grow, the company will have to create new .... , not just exploit existing
   ....
3 We need to minimize .... and ....
4 To remain ahead of the competition we will need to anticipate .... such as increased raw material costs.

3.3 Correct the mistakes using words and expressions from A and B opposite.

1 The brand is very strengthened.
2 Today, competitor fears about health are one of the biggest threats to the processed food sector.
3 An undifferentiated offer will weakness the company in the short term.
4 A clear opportunity is a gape in the market.
5 We may be threated by the emerging trend towards online shopping.
6 A war of prices has weakened our profitability.

Over to you

Think about the company you work for, or one you would like to work for. Carry out a SWOT analysis of the company. Do the same for a company you would never want to work for.

4 Marketing strategy and the marketing plan

A Marketing strategy vs. marketing plan

A company's **marketing strategy** describes how it will position itself and the **products** it **sells** or the **services** it **provides** in the **competitive marketplace**. The strategy includes a discussion of target markets, product and pricing policies, and proposed marketing and promotional initiatives (see Units 1–2 for more about the **marketing mix**).

The company's **marketing plan** is the written document which details the **marketing methods** selected (advertising, price promotions, etc.) and specific **marketing actions** or **marketing activities** (for example, a back-to-school promotional offer). It also examines the **resources** needed (both financial and human) to achieve specified **marketing objectives**, such as an increase in sales or a successful product launch, over a given period of time.

B Developing the marketing plan

You can **develop a marketing plan** using the stages known as **AOSTC** (Analysis, Objectives, Strategies, Tactics and Control).

Analysis	Current market situation	Information on the competitors and the marketplace.
	Competitor analysis	The competition in the marketplace. You will also need to include information on their **positioning** – how they control the way the customers see the products or services.
	Product / service analysis	What you sell or provide, and your **Unique Selling Point (USP)** – that is, what distinguishes your product or service from others on the market. Originally USP stood for Unique Selling Proposition, a concept developed by Rosser Reeves in the 1940s.
	Target market	Your **customer groups** or **segments** – for example, teenagers or business people (see Unit 19).
Objectives	Marketing **goals**	What you want to achieve, in terms of image and sales.
	Set **SMART** objectives	■ **Specific** – Be precise about what you are going to achieve. ■ **Measurable** – Quantify your objectives. ■ **Achievable** – Are you attempting too much? ■ **Realistic** – Do you have the resources to make the objective happen (manpower, money, machines, materials, minutes)? ■ **Timed** – When will you achieve the objective? (Within a month? By February 2015?)
Strategies	The approach to meeting the objectives	■ Which **market segment**? ■ How will we target the segment? ■ How should we position within the segment?
Tactics	Convert your strategy into the marketing mix, including the 4 Ps	■ Product ■ Price ■ Place ■ Promotion
Control	Tracking	How the success of the marketing plan will be measured (see Unit 24). How each marketing activity will be assessed.

A summary of the marketing plan, known as the **executive summary,** is included at the beginning of the document. For a list of questions to ask when preparing a marketing plan, see Appendix II on page 109.

4.1 Make word combinations with *market* and *marketing* using words from the box. Then match the word combinations with the definitions below. Look at the page opposite and Appendix II on page 109 to help you.

methods	mix	plan	segments	strategy	target

....

(**market**)

....

(**marketing**)

....
....
....
....

1 groups of consumers with similar needs or purchasing desires
2 the consumers, clients or customers you want to attract
3 a definition of the company, the product / service and the competition
4 detailed information about how to fulfil the marketing strategy
5 the techniques you can use to communicate with your consumers
6 the combination of different elements used to market a product or service

4.2 You are preparing some slides for a presentation of next year's marketing plan. Choose a title from the box for each image. Look at B opposite to help you.

Competitor Analysis	Target Market	USP

1

3

2

Over to you

Think about a product or service that you use every day. Answer the questions from Appendix II on page 109 in relation to this product or service.

5 Marketing ethics

A

Social marketing

Social marketing is the use of marketing techniques to **convince** people to change their behaviour for their own good or for the benefit of society. Encouraging smokers to stop smoking or persuading people to eat more fresh fruit and vegetables are examples. The aim of social marketing is to minimize **social problems** such as crime or poverty.

B

Corporate social responsibility (CSR)

The advantages for a company of being **socially responsible** – that is, taking positive actions for the benefit of its staff and society as a whole – include enhanced brand image, and greater ease in attracting staff. There are different ways for a company to show **corporate social responsibility (CSR)**.

- **Cause related marketing (CRM)** is when a company **donates money to a charity**, a **non-profit organization** or a good cause, such as UNICEF or Oxfam. The brand is then associated with the charity. For example, a US non-profit wild cat sanctuary, Big Cat Rescue, wants to create a **marketing partnership** with another organization:

http://www.bigcatrescue.org

Big Cat Rescue is looking for the right **corporate partner** for a **mutually beneficial** cause related marketing campaign. We need financial **donations** to be able to afford to make our good work more effective. Today most of this **funding** comes from private individuals. We are looking for a corporate partner that **shares our principles and values**.

Note: The abbreviation **CRM** also refers to Customer Relationship Management – see Unit 23.

- **Green marketing** is the development and distribution of **eco-friendly**, or **environmentally friendly**, goods – for example, washing powder that is not harmful to the environment.

6 degrees.ca is a Canadian web-based forum that promotes green marketing and **environmental protection**:

6 degrees.ca believes that if a business is behaving in an **ethical** or moral way then they will contribute to **environmental sustainability**. **Sustainable development** is development that meets the needs of today without compromising the ability of future generations to meet their needs. Responsible citizens are aware of **environmental concerns** such as global warming, and act to **protect the environment**.

- **Responsible purchasing** is another way that a company can **build** or **maintain a good reputation**. Companies can refuse to buy materials or goods made using **child labour** or that have been **tested on animals**. As well as showing concern for **human rights** and **animal testing**, a company can implement a policy of **sustainable purchasing** and only buy products that come from renewable sources.

5.1 Make word combinations using a word from each box. Two words can be used twice. Look at A and B opposite to help you.

animal	beneficial
donate	money
environmental	problems
mutually	purchasing
responsible	responsible
social	sustainability
socially	testing

5.2 Complete the texts describing examples of CSR. Then decide whether the companies are involved in CRM, green marketing or social marketing. Look at A and B opposite to help you.

a

In 2008, we are proud to continue our marketing (1) .... with the Arlette Foundation. We will promote the (2) .... in our stores and we will sell a range of products displaying the charity's distinctive logo.

.... , we will .... oney to the Arlette .... inimum .... £250,000. We are ...... (5) ....

b

The Push Play campaign in New Zealand has successfully (6) .... New Zealanders to do more exercise. The campaign aimed to limit the twin epidemics of obesity and diabetes, (7) .... problems now affecting countries worldwide.

c

CASE STUDY: *Woody Pens – Designed for the Environment*

Instead of making its pens from plastic, Goodkind Pen Company uses wood scraps from local furniture makers, and its pens are designed to be refillable.

By carefully designing its product to be eco-(8) .... and of high quality, it is mutually (9) .... for the environment and the consumer. Goodkind has made a product with a super-green profile and, in the process, enjoys a high level of satisfaction from environmentally conscious consumers and companies with a responsible (10) .... policy. Goodkind embraces environmental (11) ....

5.3 Complete the table with words from A and B opposite and related forms. Put a stress mark in front of the stressed syllable in each word. The first one has been done for you.

Noun	Adjective	Adverb
en'vironment		
		responsibly
society		socially
		sustainably

Over to you

Think about the brands you buy. How does ethical marketing influence your purchasing decisions?

6 The market environment

The micro environment

Learnmarketing.net provides information for marketing students. Its website says the following about the **micro environment**:

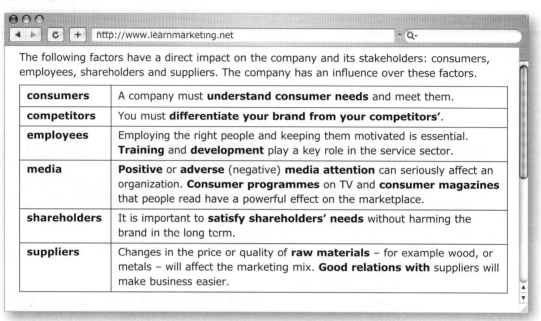

The following factors have a direct impact on the company and its stakeholders: consumers, employees, shareholders and suppliers. The company has an influence over these factors.

consumers	A company must **understand consumer needs** and meet them.
competitors	You must **differentiate your brand from your competitors'**.
employees	Employing the right people and keeping them motivated is essential. **Training** and **development** play a key role in the service sector.
media	**Positive** or **adverse** (negative) **media attention** can seriously affect an organization. **Consumer programmes** on TV and **consumer magazines** that people read have a powerful effect on the marketplace.
shareholders	It is important to **satisfy shareholders' needs** without harming the brand in the long term.
suppliers	Changes in the price or quality of **raw materials** – for example wood, or metals – will affect the marketing mix. **Good relations with** suppliers will make business easier.

The macro environment: STEP analysis

A **STEP analysis** (also known as a **PEST analysis**) looks at **sociological, technological, economic** and **political** factors in the market environment on a **macro** level – often looking at a particular country or region. The relationship between the company and these factors is indirect. This is a STEP analysis for an online supermarket in Britain.

SOCIOLOGICAL FACTORS
Dominant **religions**: Mainly Christian, with significant minorities in some regions.
Special diets in some areas.
Leisure activities: Watching TV, cooking, socializing.
Gender roles: Now that younger men shop as much as women, we need to target both sexes equally.
Birth rates: Birth rates are continuing to decline, with fewer babies born every year.
Average life expectancy: This is increasing so we should think about products for older customers.
Attitudes to foreign products: Consumers like to experiment with foreign food and drink.
Opinions on environmental issues: We should use only recyclable packaging and hybrid-fuel delivery vans.

TECHNOLOGICAL FACTORS
Innovation and technological advances:
Production: New product lines and product types are continually coming onto the market.
Offer: We now offer a new service – ordering by mobile phone.
Distribution: Online ordering has changed the way supermarkets operate. We no longer need actual shops.
Communication with consumers: Broadband internet connections make it possible to include more product photos on our site. We could even think about adding video.

ECONOMIC FACTORS
The economic forecast is good:
Interest rates: stable at 5%
Unemployment rate: less than 9% of people are out work
GDP (Gross Domestic Product): growing steadily

POLITICAL FACTORS
Political stability: Very good. Consumers feel relaxed about the political situation and ready to use consumer credit.
New tax / business legislation: No changes to the law for our business sector in the near future.
International trade agreements: We can import products from the EU without paying extra import duties.

6.1 Decide whether the following market environment characteristics are micro factors or macro factors. Look at A and B opposite to help you.

	Micro	Macro
1 High unemployment in a region reduces spending on leisure activities.		
2 The internet has opened up new distribution and marketing channels.		
3 Good relations between a supplier and a company mean that goods are always delivered on time.		
4 Legislation in European countries is restricting the right to smoke in public places.		
5 Positive reports in the national press about a brand.		
6 The staff for the telephone hotline of an internet bank are trained to be polite and friendly.		
7 During the FIFA World Cup, more snack food is consumed in front of the TV set.		

6.2 Complete the action plans (1–6) and then match them with the micro factors (a–f). Look at A opposite to help you. The first one has been done for you.

1 Convince shareholders that the best way to ......*satisfy*...... their needs in the long term is to invest in research and development.
2 Carry out market research to better .... needs and desires.
3 Prepare a press release for a .... magazine about the launch of a new product.
4 Build and maintain good .... by always paying on time.
5 Do a SWOT analysis to assess how to .... your brand from your competitors'.
6 Implement a training and .... plan to motivate and keep good members.

a competitors   c employees   e shareholders
b consumers   d media   f suppliers

6.3 Complete the STEP analysis of France. Look at B opposite to help you.

France is a member of the European Union and as such has trade (1) .... with the other members. It has one of the worst unemployment (2) .... in Europe and the government is keen to bring this down.

France has one of the highest (3) .... rates in Europe (1.9 children per woman) and a large proportion of French mothers go back to work, reflecting changes in (4) .... roles. Men are almost as likely as women to do the shopping for the family and take care of the children.

The dominant (5) .... is Catholicism, but there is a large Muslim community. The religious beliefs do not significantly affect the marketplace, except at Christmas and Easter time when the demand for Christmas trees and chocolate increases dramatically.

Internet penetration is high: most households own a computer and have high speed internet access. This has opened up new channels of (6) .... and there are now several internet grocery stores.

Nearly all teenagers own a mobile phone and they are increasingly using SMS messages to keep in touch with their peers. Marketing campaigns are beginning to exploit this line of (7) .... by sending SMS messages to their audience.

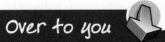

Over to you

Prepare a STEP analysis for the country or region you live in.

7 Legal aspects of marketing

A Legal definitions

The World Intellectual Property Organization gives the following definitions:

Intellectual property refers to creations of the mind: inventions, literary and artistic works, and symbols, names, images and designs used in commerce. Intellectual property is divided into two categories:

1 **Industrial property** includes **patents**, which give the **exclusive right** to make, use and sell an invention in a given geographical area; **trademarks** (words or symbols that differentiate a company); and industrial designs. A **granted patent** gives **patent protection** for 20 years in the UK. After that time you must **renew the patent**. In order to **trademark**, or **register your trademark**, you will need to complete a registration process.
2 **Copyright protects** literary and artistic works. **Copyright protected work** includes novels, plays, films, musical works, artistic works such as drawings, photographs, and architectural designs. Copyright protected work is said to be **subject to copyright**.

Note: The copyright symbol: ©
      The trademark symbol: ™
      The registered trademark symbol: ®

B Legal problems

Legal problems may arise if another person has used copyright protected work without the **copyright owner's** (or **holder's**) permission. The UK Patent Office says:

'**Intellectual property (IP) crimes** include **counterfeiting** and **piracy**. Counterfeiting is deliberate or **wilful trademark infringement** and piracy is **wilful copyright infringement**. Infringement means **reproducing copyrighted work** without permission from the **IP owner**.'

If a trademark or copyright holder believes that another person has **made unauthorized use of** a trademark or copyright, then this may lead to a **lawsuit**, where one company takes another to court to **enforce the trademark** or **copyright**. The **infringer**, the person who has broken the copyright, may have to **pay damages** or **compensation** to the trademark holder, normally financial.

Most company websites include a page called **terms and conditions** or **copyright information**. Visitors to the site must **agree to the terms and conditions**. The terms and conditions usually contain what a visitor may **download** or take from the web page and **post** or **upload** to the web page, and a **disclaimer** to say the company is not legally responsible for the misuse of its web pages.

C The Consumer Protection Act

The **Consumer Protection Act** is a law in the UK that protects the consumer from faulty or **defective products**, or products that are not as safe as they are generally expected to be. Consumers are **legally entitled to** goods of a **satisfactory quality**. Producers, suppliers and importers are **liable for** – that is, responsible for – the products they sell. Death, **personal injury** – involving physical **damage** to a person – and damage to **private property** are covered under the act.

Enforcement of the act – that is, making sure the act is respected – is the job of the **trading standards officer**. Businesses need to monitor and control their produce to make sure they are **fulfilling**, or carrying out, all **safety regulations**.

A central part of the law is **product liability**, which means that any person who is **injured** or physically hurt by a defective product does not have to **prove a manufacturer negligent** – that is, at fault – before **suing**, or taking the manufacturer to court.

7.1 Complete the copyright information from the WWF-UK web page. Look at A and B opposite to help you.

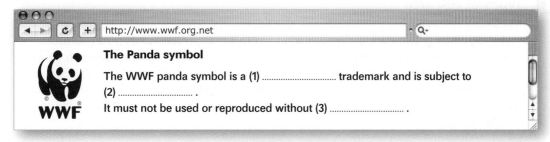

The Panda symbol

The WWF panda symbol is a (1) .... trademark and is subject to (2) ....

It must not be used or reproduced without (3) ....

7.2 Make sentences using one part from each column. Look at A and B opposite to help you.

1 Patent	must read and agree to the terms	renewed regularly.
2 A granted	protection gives a company the exclusive	to a lawsuit.
3 Wilful trademark	copyright cannot be used without	right to market a product.
4 Visitors to the website	patent must be	permission.
5 Material that is subject to	infringement may lead	and conditions.

7.3 Complete the newspaper report and then match the problems (a–c) with the offered solutions (i–iii). Look at C opposite to help you.

FIGHT FOR YOUR RIGHTS WHEN A DEAL GOES WRONG

By Ruki Sayid

Stores do their best to part us from our cash, but they are not always as friendly if a (1) .... is defective. We have teamed up with consumer watchdog *Which?* to offer some help.

a   The iron I bought was faulty and I was given a replacement, but that also stopped working after a week. The shop has refused to exchange it, saying the second iron was a gift. Is this correct?

b   My parents bought us a washing machine as a present but it exploded when we were out. The smoke and fire damage is extensive. Who is responsible for this?

c   I have written many letters to a local supermarket after having found bits of glass in their fresh fruit. I still don't have a satisfactory response.

Which? **answers:**

i   As you did not buy the machine yourself, you have no contract with the shop. But you can claim against the manufacturer under the Consumer Protection Act 1987 for (2) .... to your house and any (3) .... injury. Your parents, however, can claim for the machine from the retailer.

ii   Try contacting the trading (4) .... officer. He / she is responsible for (5) .... of the Consumer Protection Act.

iii   No, you are legally (6) .... to goods of a (7) .... quality.

Over to you

Think about intellectual property owned by your business, school or family. What is it, and how is it protected?

8 Research 1

A
A Types of research

Marketing research is the process of gathering information about a market, analysing it and interpreting it. Although the term **market research** is often used to mean the same thing, technically it only refers to research into a specific market. **Consumer research** – used to discover **behaviour patterns** (how people act) and **customer needs** (see Unit 20) – is an essential element of marketing research. **Motivation research** investigates the psychological reasons why individuals buy specific types of merchandise, or why they respond to specific advertising appeals.

There are two main methods of consumer research:

- **desk (desktop) research** or **secondary research**: an analysis of the information you can find easily without leaving your desk. Examples include the internet, books, newspapers, magazines, and government statistics.

- **field research** or **primary research**: involves talking to people and finding out what they think about a market, a product, a business sector, etc. It is usually **carried out** by market research institutes.

Consumer research can be either **qualitative** or **quantitative**. In qualitative research, small **group discussions** or **in-depth interviews** with consumers are used to understand a problem better. Quantitative research involves **collecting**, or **gathering**, large **samples of data** (for example, on how many people use different products), followed by **statistical analysis** – examining, or **analysing**, the data. Quantitative research is often used to investigate the findings from qualitative research.

Note: The singular noun is (an) **analysis**, and the plural is **analyses**. **Data** is used as both an uncountable noun and as a plural noun. *The data is interesting. The data show interesting trends.* The activity of **analysing data** can also be referred to as **mining data**.

B
B Research methodology

A student has made notes while reading a book on marketing research techniques.

Focus groups: small groups from the target group plus one moderator to mediate or run the session. The moderator prepares questions for the session.

Package test: used to test ideas for new packaging; could be in a focus group.

Taste test: used to test what consumers think about new flavours.

Home test: consumers try the products at home, in a real situation.

A self-administered questionnaire is completed (or filled in) by the respondent, and an interviewer-administered questionnaire is filled in on behalf of the respondent by an interviewer.

Telephone surveys are carried out by telephoning the respondent and asking questions.

A mail survey is mailed to the respondent, who completes it and posts it back.

Online surveys are administered on the internet.

Mystery shopping: a person poses as a consumer and checks the level of service and hygiene in a restaurant, hotel or shop.

Omnibus surveys: a market research institute carries out (or conducts) research for several companies at the same time. A long survey is given to respondents; some institutes have a panel of existing respondents who are accustomed to answering the surveys.

8.1 Match the types of research in the box with the research problems below. Look at A and B opposite to help you.

desktop + secondary	qualitative + field
motivation + primary	quantitative + primary

1 The R&D department want to know why people buy mobile phones so that they can develop a new model that answers all the major needs.
2 The design team want to know how consumers feel about the new layout of the company website before they finalize and launch the new homepage.
3 A manager wants to have financial data on her company, her competitors and the economy in general.
4 The marketing team want to have a lot of data on their consumers: age, shopping habits, email address, etc.

8.2 Complete the sentences. Look at B opposite to help you.

1 A lot of marketing research institutes carry out .... surveys. They ring people at home and ask them questions.
2 A .... is a small discussion group, led by a .... who asks questions to get detailed and qualitative information.
3 A marketing research institute may prepare a lengthy .... survey which it posts to consumers at their homes. These .... surveys have questions from several different companies on them.
4 Some questionnaires are completed by the .... (self-administered questionnaires) and some are completed by the interviewer (................................-................................ questionnaires).
5 .... surveys are usually carried out in-store to assess the levels of service quality and cleanliness.
6 A .... test is designed to find out what consumers think about packaging, and a .... test is to find out what they think about the flavour of a product.

8.3 Cross out the incorrect sentence in each group. Look at A and B opposite to help you.

1
a We carried out the research last week.
b We conducted the research last week.
c We collected the research last week.

2
a The respondents completed a questionnaire.
b The respondents analysed a questionnaire.
c The respondents filled in a questionnaire.

3
a We must run the data quickly.
b We must collect the data quickly.
c We must gather the data quickly.

4
a It can take a long time to mine data.
b It can take a long time to carry out data.
c It can take a long time to analyse data.

5
a We are filling in three focus groups.
b We are mediating three focus groups.
c We are running three focus groups.

Over to you

Think about how you would carry out market research for a completely new product (for example, a light bulb that works without electricity). What kind of research would you conduct during the development phase of the product, and what kind just before the product launch?

9 Research 2

A ## Describing survey results

There are number of different ways to talk about survey results.

Recent research The survey The latest figures The key findings	highlight(s) indicate(s) reveal(s) show(s) suggest(s)	the need to ... that the respondents feel strongly about ... that the **trend** is **upward** ↑ / **downward** ↓ ... **satisfaction with** the service – people are happy with it. **dissatisfaction with** the product range – people don't like it. **that our consumers would prefer to** see ...

A mere 5% **Ten percent** **Over** half **Almost** 60% **Nearly** two thirds	of the respondents	**said** taste was very important. **claimed** taste influenced their purchase. **cited** taste **as an important part of** the decision to buy. **rated** the new taste better than the old one. **thought** the taste was much better.

Note: The **key findings** are the most important findings.
We use **mere** when we want to emphasize that the amount is not large, or not important.
For more information on talking about figures see Appendix III on page 110.

B ## Understanding trends and changes

Maggie Potters has just completed a survey of consumer ratings for a brand of mobile phones and is making a presentation to the phone manufacturers.

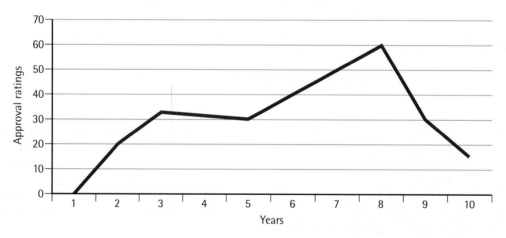

'The **graph** shows consumer ratings of the product **over a ten-year period.** You can see that after the launch of the product the ratings **rose to** 33%. The trend was **stable** until the arrival of a major competitor in the market. This led to a **slight fall** in approval ratings. The relaunch of the brand invigorated the product and so you can see ratings **rising to** 60%, the ratings **doubled.** However, reports in the national press have had a negative effect on the brand image and approval ratings have **plummeted.** Compared to **the same period last year,** a **significantly** higher number of consumers have a low opinion of the product and the brand image. The percentage of dissatisfied respondents has **trebled.** Although this seems to be very negative, your initial **guesstimates,** your predictions before you had the figures, were much worse.'

9.1 Read the extract from a survey of blog readers by Blogads, and correct any mistakes in the sentences below. Look at A opposite and Appendix III on page 110 to help you.

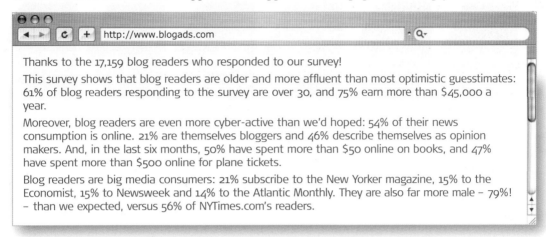

Thanks to the 17,159 blog readers who responded to our survey!

This survey shows that blog readers are older and more affluent than most optimistic guesstimates: 61% of blog readers responding to the survey are over 30, and 75% earn more than $45,000 a year.

Moreover, blog readers are even more cyber-active than we'd hoped: 54% of their news consumption is online. 21% are themselves bloggers and 46% describe themselves as opinion makers. And, in the last six months, 50% have spent more than $50 online on books, and 47% have spent more than $500 online for plane tickets.

Blog readers are big media consumers: 21% subscribe to the New Yorker magazine, 15% to the Economist, 15% to Newsweek and 14% to the Atlantic Monthly. They are also far more male – 79%! – than we expected, versus 56% of NYTimes.com's readers.

1 Three quarters of the respondents earn more than $45,000 a year.
2 Almost half of their news consumption is online.
3 A mere 79% of respondents are male.
4 One out of two respondents has spent more than $50 online on books.
5 The survey suggests that all bloggers are over 30.

9.2 Complete the description of the graph. Look at B opposite to help you.

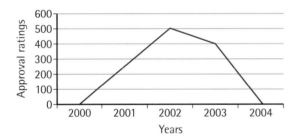

The graph represents intentions to buy (1) .... a five-year period. The new insurance policy was launched in 2000. After the launch, the intention to buy (2) .... sharply. A (3) .... higher number of consumers expressed a strong interest in the policy. This upward trend was (4) .... for a two-year (5) .... In 2003 the company started to suffer from a damaged reputation, following allegations of illegal trading on the stock market. This is reflected in the number of intentions to buy, which (6) .... just before the company name was changed and the policy dropped.

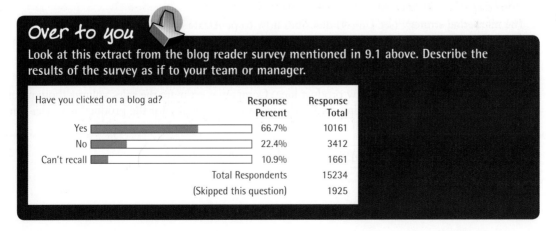

Over to you

Look at this extract from the blog reader survey mentioned in 9.1 above. Describe the results of the survey as if to your team or manager.

Have you clicked on a blog ad?	Response Percent	Response Total
Yes	66.7%	10161
No	22.4%	3412
Can't recall	10.9%	1661
Total Respondents		15234
(Skipped this question)		1925

10 New product development 1

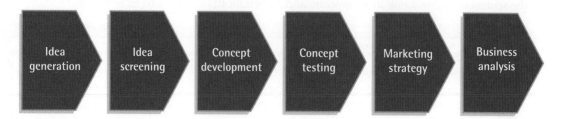

Idea generation → Idea screening → Concept development → Concept testing → Marketing strategy → Business analysis

A Idea generation

Idea generation is the systematic search for **new product ideas**. It is the first step in the **new product development (NPD)** process. NPD is essential for companies to **stay competitive**. Ideas for **product innovation** can come from many sources – for example, internal brainstorming (see Unit 12), distributors, or increasingly from customers. Many companies are adopting a **customer-driven** or **customer-centric** marketing approach, focused on **identifying customer demands** (what customers are asking for) and understanding **consumer needs** (what customers require to solve a particular problem). Market research techniques (see Unit 8) are used to **identify gaps in the market**.

Throughout the NPD process, marketers work closely with **research and development (R&D)** to create original products or to modify or improve existing products. **New recipes** (for example, Vanilla Coke) and **limited** or **special editions** (for example, Christmas tea) are examples of **product improvements** and **product modifications**. The product innovation may target a **mass market** or a specific **niche market** – products for left-handed people, for example.

B Idea screening

Launching new products is a risky business, so new product ideas are **screened** to select, or **spot, potentially successful product ideas**. A company has to assess which ideas are **viable** (will survive in a competitive marketplace), **technically feasible** (the company has the skills and resources to produce them), and **profitable** (will make money). The company also considers **overall demand** – how much they can expect to sell.

C Concept development and testing

An attractive idea is developed into several different product concepts. **Concept testing** measures **customer response** to a new product – what customers think of it – and gives an indication of the **level of consumer acceptance** – that is, how readily consumers will use the product. The objective is to successfully introduce the new product onto the market or **penetrate the market**, and to **minimize the research and development costs**.

D Marketing strategy and business analysis

The marketing strategy (see Unit 4) describes how to penetrate the market. You must decide which **route to market** is best for your product or service. You can **produce** it yourself, you can **sell the idea**, or you can **license the product to** another company to produce and market.

Before moving on to the **product development phase** (see Unit 11), businesses need to assess the financial attractiveness of the new product idea. Companies estimate the **sales volume** (how much they will be able to sell), the **selling price** (what consumers will pay for the product or service) and **revenue expectations** (how much income the product will generate).

> BrE: licence (noun), license (verb); AmE: license (noun), license (verb)

10.1 Find words and phrases in A, B, C and D opposite to make word combinations with the words below.

product ....   market

10.2 Complete the sentences about new product ideas. Look at A and B opposite to help you.

1 A .... edition pack could be good to celebrate the fiftieth anniversary of the product.
2 We must be responsive and ....-driven. Have we identified the customer needs and demands?
3 A .... recipe would work well for a short time, but does it really show added value?
4 I don't think that would be .... feasible. We just couldn't produce it.
5 Is that really going to work? I mean, is it really .... in our marketplace?

10.3 Complete the text. Look at A, B, C and D opposite to help you.

⊖ ○ ○

Here's how I exploited a (1) .... in the market

Gecko Headgear Ltd is a designer and manufacturer of marine safety helmets, founded in 1993 by Jeff Sacrée. Jeff explains how he spotted a gap in the niche water sports (2) ....

'As a surfer, I could see a potentially (3) .... product, a helmet that was both lightweight and heat-retaining.'

'However, surfing is a relatively small market and I began wondering if I could (4) .... other markets with my helmet design.'

Jeff adds, 'A good relationship with the bank is crucial when you're trying to bring an innovative product to market. In our case the product (5) .... phase took three years – far longer than we initially expected.' Jeff decided the best (6) .... to market was to grow his business and produce the helmets himself.

Over to you

Imagine you are talking to Steve Jobs at Apple about his next i-product. Think of three questions to ask him about the product. Think of three more questions you could use to screen his ideas.

11 New product development 2

Product development & optimization   Test marketing   Commercialization

A Workflow

Companies need to organize their **workflow** efficiently to move quickly through the new product development process and **beat the competitors to market** – that is, get to market first with a **successful product launch**. Efficient product development processes increase the chance of doing well, or **likelihood of success**. The amount of time a new product or service spends **in the development pipeline** – or how long it takes to develop – is referred to as **time to market**.

During the process, the **project team**, made up of a **project leader** and the people needed to complete the project, completes **key activities** (for example, carrying out market research) to advance the project and collects information to **manage risk** – to make decisions that will reduce the risk of failure in the future. **Prioritization decisions** are made to identify the most important things to do next and **resources** are **allocated** to the best projects. An **action plan**, a list of what needs to be done next, is defined.

B Product development and optimization

Clay model of a new car design

Many product concepts exist only as a description – a drawing, or a very basic model known as a **mock-up**. For example, car makers prepare clay models of new car designs. **Product modelling** uses **CAD** (computer aided design) to turn ideas into **3D representations**. The R&D team **creates a prototype**, a first example of the product, to test its functionality and to eliminate **product flaws**. **Prototyping** helps cut costs and allows for market testing.

For software, the first stage is an **alpha test**, where the program is tested by company employees to remove any errors, or **bugs**. Then the software is sent for external testing; this is known as **beta testing**.

Product optimization studies are **carried out** to **improve** the product or service as it is being developed. They may include **sensory research** to evaluate how a product smells, tastes or feels.

C Test marketing

The next step is to collect information on how the proposed product or service will **perform in the marketplace**. The company tests the product and its marketing plan on a small **test market** before a **full launch**. This allows the company to **forecast** or predict **sales, uncover problems** with the product, and to **fine-tune**, or adjust, the marketing plan (see Unit 4). The amount and type of testing depends on the **costs and risks** of introducing the product.

D Commercialization

Commercialization, also known as **market introduction**, is the final stage in the new product development process. The **distribution network** and **marketing communications action plan** must be ready by the **launch date** or **commercialization date** – the date the product goes on sale. The company may launch the product simultaneously in all markets or prepare a step-by-step **market rollout** in different cities and countries.

Note: For more on distribution, see Unit 26.
For more on publicity and promotion, see Units 32–43.

11.1 Make sentences using one part from each column. Then match the sentences (1–5) with the stages of the development process (a–c). Look at B, C and D opposite to help you.

1 We should carry	date and now need to prepare the distribution	plan.
2 We have completed the alpha	rollout across	research.
3 The results will allow us to fine-	test and are now ready for beta	network.
4 We have planned the market	tune our marketing	testing.
5 We have set a launch	out some sensory	Europe.

a test marketing
b commercialization
c product development and optimization

11.2 Complete the description of product development using words from the box. Look at A, B, C and D opposite to help you.

date	forecast	manage	prototype	resources	time
flaws	launch	product	representations	success	

After we get the OK for the product concept we need to allocate (1) .... to the next stage: product development. We start by (2) .... modelling. We have to create a (3) .... which we use to identify and eliminate product (4) .... in order to increase the likelihood of (5) .... We use CAD to create 3D (6) .... Although there is always pressure to reduce our (7) .... to market, I think it is important to (8) .... risk well so that the product launch is a success. At the end of the product development and optimization stage, the project moves into test marketing, used to (9) .... sales. In the last project we worked on, we carried out a test of the market before the full (10) .... At the end, a commercialization (11) .... is set and the product is launched, successfully we hope.

11.3 Correct the mistakes in the sentences about the launch of PS3, Sony's gaming console, using words from A, B and D opposite.

1 PS3 spent a long time in the development pipe.
2 The marketing introduction stage did not go smoothly for PS3.
3 The original launch day for PS3 was in the spring.
4 The action rollout in Europe for PS3 was delayed.
5 The launch event in France was a failure because the marketing communications test plan was poorly prepared.
6 Sony is also launching an international e-distribution net to provide online content.

Over to you

Present the different stages of product development. Use a fictional or real product to illustrate your talk.

12 Brainstorming

A The brainstorming session

Brainstorming is a technique used by marketers during **product naming** to find new names for products, or during **product development** (see Unit 10) to find new products and to **generate ideas**.

There are three roles for **participants** in a **brainstorming team**: leader, scribe and team members.

Before the session, the leader needs to define a **problem statement** – for example, 'how to sell more of our biscuits'. The problem statement needs to **focus on** the aim of the session, but it must be open enough to allow **innovative thinking**.

The leader must also **set the ground rules** for brainstorming:

- All ideas are welcome. During **brainstorming** sessions, no **judgements** or **criticisms** should be **made** of ideas. Do not **criticize ideas**. Do not **evaluate ideas**. They can be **modified** later.
- Change involves **risk-taking**, so it's important to be open to original ideas. The **quantity of ideas** (how many there are) is more important than the **quality** (how good they are).
- There is **no ownership of ideas** – the ideas belong to the group. Participants should 'hitchhike' on, or **build on**, other people's **creative ideas**.

The scribe needs to write down, or **note down**, every idea – clearly, where all the team members can see them.

B Brainstorming techniques

You may need to **get the creative juices flowing** (get people thinking more creatively), and encourage people to **think out of the box** – look at a problem from a new or different angle.

One common technique is to use a **random word** as a **starting point** for possible solutions. There are many **random word generators** on the internet.

Michael Michalko is a creative thinking expert. He uses a technique called **combinatory play**. Random words are listed and then put together. You play with the **combinations** until you find a promising new combination. For example, suntan lotion and insect repellent **combine** to form a new product – one lotion that protects against both the sun and insects.

One final technique is to **ask novel questions** (new or different questions) that will stimulate creative answers, for example: 'Which noises do you associate with pencils?' or 'What other uses do people have for pencils?'

C Suggesting and building on ideas

During a brainstorming session for the name of a new toothpaste, the brainstorming team say the following things:

> **This is probably crazy, but what about** using an animal name for the paste?

> Interesting suggestion. **Let's go back to Sally's idea** about using the word 'cool'.

> 'Cool White' is a good name. **It makes me think of** white teeth.

> It's a bit obvious, isn't it? **Just a suggestion – couldn't we try** a different colour? Blue perhaps?

> **I've got it!** I have the perfect solution.

> If we combine your idea with Sally's, we'll have 'Cool Blue'.

12.1 Choose the correct words from the brackets to complete the brainstorming rules. Look at A and B opposite to help you.

1 It's a (brainstormer / brainstorming / brainstorm) session. The purpose is to (generate / evaluate / generalize) ideas.
2 Please don't (criticize / define / diagnose) or judge the quality of other people's ideas.
3 We're looking for quantity, rather than quality. We can (modernize / moderate / modify) ideas later.
4 Build (up / over / on) each other's ideas. It is this building of ideas that leads to (outer / out of / over) the box thinking and fantastic ideas.

12.2 Complete the sentences (1–4), and then match each sentence with the participant who says it in a brainstorming session (a–c). Look at C opposite to help you.

1

Hey, I've .... it!

3

I've noted .... all the ideas. Thanks, everyone.

2

Thanks, John. Let's go .... to Peter's idea about the ...

4

OK everyone, try to stay focused .... the problem.

a the leader
b the scribe
c a team member

12.3 Match the two parts of the sentences from a brainstorming session. Look at A and B opposite to help you.

1 I'd like to remind you all of the ground
2 I hope you've been thinking about the problem
3 Today we need innovative
4 Don't be afraid to take
5 So, the random
6 Thanks for a very productive brainstorming

a risks – no one will criticize you.
b session.
c word is 'butter'.
d statement I emailed you.
e rules before we start.
f thinking for a new product name.

12.4 A company called Speechmark is brainstorming ideas for the title of their internal newsletter. Complete the sentences. Look at C opposite to help you.

1 Today we're looking for a two-word title for the newsletter. You all know the .... rules – let's get started.
2 Here's a list of keywords to get your creative .... flowing.
3 .... we use the company name in the title?
4 Good suggestion. What .... the other word?
5 Just a .... – couldn't we try 'inside'?
6 I like that – it .... me think about being at home.
7 So, if I .... those two ideas, we'll have 'Speechmark Inside'.

Over to you

Brainstorm a new product for the silver market (see Appendix V on page 112). Use a random word generator from the internet to help you get your creative juices flowing.

13 Product and service types

A Product types

Raw materials – such as cotton, gold and oil – are used to make, or **manufacture**, other products. A group of related products made and marketed by a **manufacturer** is a **product line**. There is usually a **logical grouping** of products – for example, Faber-Castell produce writing instruments, both high quality pencils for children and adults, and also high quality pens. A **product type** is a group of products **offered** by different companies which are technically similar. However, there will be variations in terms of price, appearance and marketing. A good example is cosmetics and make-up. A **product class** is a group of products that may be considered as substitutes for one another. H&M and Zara clothes are in the same class. Christian Dior is the same product type but not in the same class.

B Word combinations with 'goods' and 'products'

convenience fast moving consumer consumer packaged	goods	= products with a high turnover and relatively low price, such as table salt or shampoo
white		= major household electrical goods which are usually white, such as freezers, washing machines and dishwashers
brown		= major household electrical goods that are not usually white, such as camcorders, televisions and DVD players
perishable		= goods that have a limited **shelf life** and must be consumed relatively quickly, such as fresh fruit, fresh meat and eggs
durable / hard		= goods that last for a long time – they cannot be easily worn out or used up, such as cars, furniture and white goods
nondurable / soft		= goods that are used up or last for less than three years – for example, perishable goods, **consumable supplies** such as CD ROMs, or ink for a printer

green	products	= products that are not harmful for the environment (see Unit 5)
generic		= products sold without a brand name, usually in a supermarket or in a pharmacy as alternatives to brand name drugs (see Unit 16)
healthcare		= products that are beneficial for your health and well-being – for example, vitamins and plasters

Note: The expressions **fast moving consumer goods** and **consumer packaged goods** are often abbreviated to **FMCG** and **CPG**. Perishable products and goods can also be called **perishables**. Durable goods can also be called **durables**.

C Types of service

A **service** is a non-material good, **provided** by a company or an individual.

Common service types are:

childcare (childminders, kindergartens)
financial (banking, real estate)
consulting (business and financial advisors)
risk management (insurance and security)
cleaning and maintenance (office cleaners, gardeners)
education and training (private schools, adult colleges)

healthcare (doctors, hospitals)
hairdressing (small salons and large groups)
telecommunications (mobile phones, fixed lines)
entertainment (cinemas, theatres)
tourism (hotels, airlines)
marketing and advertising (consultancies and agencies)

13.1 Complete the magazine article. Look at A opposite to help you.

Artificial diamonds may outsparkle genuine articles

Diamonds, one of the world's most beautiful and sought-after (1) .... , are now facing stiff competition from artificial gems.

Apollo Diamonds, based in Boston, and Florida-based Gemesis both (2) .... artificial diamonds with equipment that replicates the high pressure and temperatures found within the earth. This new (3) ....

is attracting interest from jewellers and (4) .... of semi-conductors.

De Beers Diamond Trading Company denies claims that the artificial diamonds are in the same (5) .... as natural diamonds. Natural gems 'have a mystique and an emotional value to them with which synthetics can never compete', said Gareth Penny, of De Beers.

13.2 Make word combinations with *goods* and *products* using words from the box. One word can be used twice. Then match the word combinations with the pictures (1–7) below. Look at B opposite to help you.

brown	convenience	hard	healthcare	nondurable	perishable	white

....
....
....
....   **goods**   ....   **products**
....
....

1
3
5
7

2
4
6

Over to you

Keep a purchasing diary for a week and note down all the product and service types you buy. Which ones do you spend most money on? Which ones do you purchase most often?

Purchasing diary

Date	Price	Quantity	Brand	Item description
12/06	£1.20	1	Danone	Four pack of natural yoghurt

14 Product life cycles

The Boston Consulting Group Matrix

The Boston Consulting Group Matrix was devised in the 1970s as a **planning tool** for marketers to help them analyse their product lines and decide where to allocate money. **Market growth rate**, the speed at which the market is expanding, is plotted against **relative market share** – the percentage of consumers in the market that buy your service or product. Products or services have either **high** or **low market growth rates** or relative market shares.

Inside the Boston Box

In the matrix, products or services are divided into four different types. They relate to four stages in the **product life cycle (PLC)**.

Note: **Problem children** are also known as **question marks**; **stars** are also known as **rising stars**.

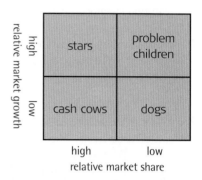

Stage of PLC	Position in the matrix
Product launch	**Problem children** are products or services that are not yet **established**, or well known, in the market. They will **consume resources** – for example, time or money – before giving a **return on investment (ROI)**. In some cases these products or services may never be **profitable** – make the company money – especially if they are in a **slow-growing** business sector or a **saturated market**, such as diet drinks or the mobile phone market.
Growth	**Stars** have both high market growth rate and high relative market share. These products or services are probably in a **fast-growing** business sector. They **generate high cash flows**, but are not always profitable. **Profitability** depends on the amount **invested** in the star.
Maturity	**Cash cows** have high relative market share, but little market growth. They are products or services that consumers know, trust and consume. They **generate profit** as they don't need much investment. They can be used to **feed research and development** for other products.
Decline	**Dogs** are products or services that have low relative market share and low market growth. They consume resources and do not create profit. They may **generate** a **negative cash flow** – that is, they **make a loss**. The best course of action is to raise prices to maximize income, known as **harvesting**, before finally **dropping the line** – taking the product or service off the market.

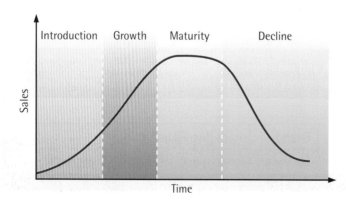

The product life cycle

14.1 Put the words in italics in the correct order to complete the sentences. Look at A and B opposite to help you.

1 *Boston Consulting Matrix The Group* is used as a planning tool.
2 It concerns the *cycle life product*.
3 A product with a *market relative high share* and *market growth rate low* is a cash cow.
4 Cash cows can be used to fund *development research and* for new products.
5 Stars may *cash high flows generate* but are not always profitable.
6 Dogs may *cash negative flow generate*.
7 It may be necessary to *line the drop*.
8 Question marks will consume resources before *a return investment on giving*.

14.2 Decide where the following services can be placed on the Boston matrix: as question mark / problem child, star, cash cow or dog. Look at B opposite to help you.

1
Network protection
Protect your network from hackers and viruses.
Contact us today for the latest in network protection.
Now over 5,000 happy clients.
Join the fastest growing safe online community.

3

Summer Sale
Book Now
Visit our online store to find reductions on weekend breaks in North Wales
Hurry: some of our hotels are being converted into private apartments
Offer ends October 31st

2
Join The Diet Club
Lose weight quickly and safely
Millions of slimmer clients
Read their testimonials
The Diet Club: trusted nutritionists delivering sound advice for generations

4
New service
You can now raise money for your favourite charities by using CharitySearchClick.com. All you need to do is use **CSC** every time you search on the web, and we will donate half our profit to your selected charity.
Try it today and tell your friends.

14.3 Find nouns and expressions in A and B opposite that can be used to make word combinations with the words below.

(generate) ....
....

(market) ....
....
....

Over to you
Search on the internet or look in a supermarket for products and services to complete a Boston Box. Try to find at least one example of a star, a problem child, a cash cow and a dog.

15 Selling products and services

A The seller

The **sales force** (see Unit 31) are the people who **sell a product** or **sell a service**. Their goal is to **close a deal** and **make a sale**. These people are trained to push back, or counter, **arguments against** their **sales pitch** (how they try to sell to you).

The general term for a person who sells for a living is **salesperson**. However, several other variations of the job title exist, depending on the job itself. For more information, see Appendix I on page 108.

B The purchaser

Type of selling		Description of purchaser and supplier
business to business	B2B	A **purchaser** (or buyer) in the **procurement department** is employed by a company to **get the best deal from their suppliers** (the lowest price or best payment terms).
		Retail buyers work for supermarkets or other types of **retail outlet**. They negotiate **retail listings** or **supermarket listings** with suppliers, meaning that the retailer agrees to list the product as something they sell. The supplier needs to **secure a listing** or **get the products listed** or the outlet will not **give shelf space** to the product – that is, display the product in the store.
business to consumer	B2C	Individual clients or customers buy from a shop or an online store (see Units 26 and 30).
consumer to consumer	C2C	Individual people sell to other individuals. The classified ads in local newspapers are a good example. C2C has become more common thanks to internet sites such as eBay.

C Selling a service

A product is **tangible**, meaning it can be touched. A service, such as business consulting or healthcare, is **intangible** and does not have a physical presence. Packaging your service to make it look like a product is a frequently used marketing technique.

A marketing student is making notes from an article offering advice on selling services:

- Package your different **service levels**. Create **bundles** that are easily sellable and that **cater to your customers'** varying **needs** and budgets. A **high-end package** for a car maintenance plan may include picking up the car for service and cleaning the interior. A **low-end, prepaid package** could include a reminder phone call for service and an oil change. These levels are differences in the **actual deliverables** and the **total value**.

- **Combine services** to **create a new offering**. For instance, as a marketing consultant, you could join forces with a copywriter and a graphic designer to create a 'Business Start-up Success' package.

service levels = differently priced levels of service, at different quality levels

bundles = services in groups that are sold together

actual deliverables = what the consumer receives, i.e. a clean car

total value = the sum of the value of the individual services in the bundle

15.1 Complete the sentences. Look at A opposite and Appendix I on page 108 to help you.

1 Our sales .... is very effective. They sell a lot of products.
2 A sales .... came to the office yesterday. I didn't like his sales .... at all – he just talked and talked and didn't listen to what I was saying.
3 I'm a sales .... I work for an insurance company in Geneva.
4 As soon as a customer walks in, I know if I am going to .... a sale.

15.2 Choose the correct words from the brackets to complete the advice for food and drink companies on the Scottish Food and Drink website. Look at B opposite to help you.

> http://www.scottishfoodanddrink.com
>
> Need to increase (1) .... (retail buyers / shelf space) to grow the business but not sure how? The first step is to secure (2) .... (a listing / an outlet), then you can target growth through increased shelf space. However, space is always at a premium and success will depend on a number of factors. Convince the (3) .... (retail buyer / procurement department) that your product is worth more space by showing him or her what other retail (4) .... (listings / outlets) in the local area are doing.

15.3 Two marketers are talking about how to market their investment services. Match the two parts of the sentences. Look at C opposite to help you.

1 Let's start by looking at turning the service into a product. Our investment services are
2 Yes, we could try to create
3 I don't know, our business is really too complicated for prepaid
4 Our clients really need us to cater
5 Well, we could think about different service
6 Do you mean high and low
7 Yes, and we could combine different services to provide a new

a bundles of different investment services.
b levels for differing budgets.
c offering. Say, life insurance, real estate, shares, bonds, savings accounts combined into one easy to manage portfolio.
d intangible so it might be an interesting approach for our clients.
e packages.
f end packages?
g to their individual budgets and needs.

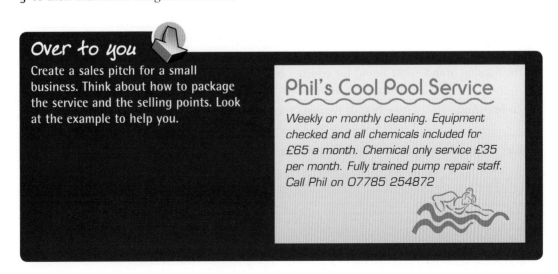

Over to you

Create a sales pitch for a small business. Think about how to package the service and the selling points. Look at the example to help you.

Phil's Cool Pool Service

Weekly or monthly cleaning. Equipment checked and all chemicals included for £65 a month. Chemical only service £35 per month. Fully trained pump repair staff. Call Phil on 07785 254872

16 Branding 1

A What is a brand?

Most companies decide to **brand** their products or services by using a name, a symbol or a design to identify it and **differentiate** it **from** the **competitive set** – that is, rival brands. Consumers can easily recognize the brand and the **brand values** – what it stands for (see Unit 18).

A **brand name** is the name given to a product or a **range** of products – goods of a similar type that are marketed together. This may be the same name as the company (for example, Coca-Cola) or it may be a different name (for example, Apple's iPod). The **trademark** is the legal protection for the brand (see Unit 7), its logo (see Unit 44) and its brand name.

B Branding

A **brand manager** is responsible for **branding** – creating, maintaining and building a brand. He or she works on all aspects of the brand:

the **brand image**	How the consumers see the brand: the values they associate with it.
the **brand essence**	One core concept which defines the brand. It is normally expressed in a short phrase or just one word. A good example is 'Volvo equals safety'.
the **brand promise**	The explicit promise the organization makes to its target audiences, including employees, about the quality and use of the brand.
the **brand vision**	The brand vision communicates where the brand is and where the brand can go. It talks about the values the brand has today and the values it will need in the future, as well as the communication tools needed to achieve this.

C Word combinations with 'brand'

a **premium brand**	a high quality brand, more expensive than its competitors
an **economy brand**	a brand that is cheaper than its competitors
an **own brand**	a brand that is made exclusively for the retailer that sells it; also known as an **own-label brand** or a **private label brand**
a **brand leader**	the best-selling brand in a particular market
a **no brand**	a product that doesn't have a brand associated with it; also known as a **generic brand**
the **flagship brand**	the brand for which a business is best known, and which represents its image most appropriately
co-branding	two brands working together to create a new product – for example, Intel Corporation and Apple Computers Inc.

Note: We can also talk about a **flagship store** or a **flagship shop**.

16.1 Complete the crossword. Look at A and C opposite to help you.

Across
2 To make your brand different from other brands. (13)
3 This type of brand is produced for and sold in supermarkets: ....-label. (3)
5 A .... brand is also known as a no brand. (7)
6 A well-known product that best represents the brand. (8)
8 A set of products grouped under the same brand. (5)
9 A type of brand that is less expensive than some similar products. (7)

Down
1 Using a name, symbol, logo or design to identify a product. (8)
4 This type of brand is luxurious and more expensive than some similar products. (7)
7 The best-selling brand in a product category is the brand .... (6)

16.2 Read what the brand manager says about the brand and identify whether she is talking about the brand image, essence, promise or vision. Look at B opposite to help you.

1
> It's fine contemporary chocolate.

2
> When the consumers buy our chocolate they are making a statement about how much they enjoy the finer things in life. It's about treating yourself to a moment of indulgence. You can share the chocolate with someone close. It's about pleasure.

3
> It's luxury, sure, but it's also really trendy and modern. In a recent survey consumers said our chocolate was 'upmarket', 'classy' and 'distinctive'.

4
> Chocolate in general is considered to be bad for your health and body. We need to convince our consumers that it can also be good. It's full of magnesium and it's nearly 80% pure cocoa content. It's a luxury product, so we will work on packaging and maybe do some artistic colour ads in glossy magazines, such as *Vogue*.

Over to you

Think about your favourite brand. Prepare a presentation of its brand image. Use information from the company's website.

17 Branding 2

A Brand platform

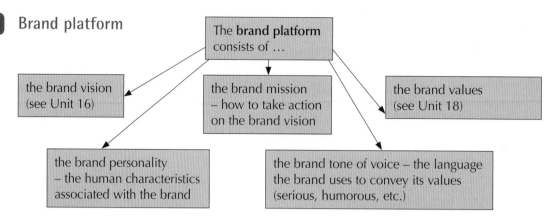

The **brand platform** consists of ...

the brand vision (see Unit 16)

the brand mission – how to take action on the brand vision

the brand values (see Unit 18)

the brand personality – the human characteristics associated with the brand

the brand tone of voice – the language the brand uses to convey its values (serious, humorous, etc.)

B Brand management

Brand management, the application of marketing techniques to a brand, was first used by Proctor and Gamble in the 1930s. The **brand strategy** (see C below) shows how the brand will meet its objectives. It influences the overall business strategy of a company to ensure consistent **brand behaviour**, meaning what the brand does and how it acts in all advertising media, and consistent **brand experience** – the exposure and interaction a consumer has with the brand. **Total branding** refers to a consistent approach to brand behaviour and brand experiences across all possible **touchpoints** – wherever the consumer has a brand experience: TV, out-of-home, at a friend's house, etc.

C Brand strategy

A marketing manager writes an email about brand strategy to his contact in a communications agency.

New Message

... Last year we **launched the brand** in a new market; this year we need to **establish the brand** and make it stronger. It's too early to **rebrand** – change the name – but we could **stretch the brand** to include holiday reservations as well as holiday insurance. This **brand extension** will help us to **market the brand** to new consumers. Our **brand positioning** of reliable holidays allows us to **enhance the brand**, improving it in this way. ...

D More word combinations with 'brand'

using **brand leverage**	using the power of a brand name or part of a brand identity (colour, similar name, typeface, etc.) to build or launch another brand
maintaining **brand equity**	protecting the value of the brand name
building **brand preference**	increasing the number of consumers who prefer the brand over another
building **brand loyalty**	making sure your consumers want to buy your brand again and again (also known as increasing **brand retention**)
building **brand awareness**	increasing the number of consumers who know about your brand
building **brand consideration**	increasing the number of consumers who consider buying your brand

17.1 Read the notes made during a brainstorming session on an online supermarket's brand platform, and say which part of the brand platform they refer to. Look at A opposite to help you.

1

Friendly
Efficient
Careful

2

Cheap
Good quality
Reliable

3

Amusing online ads
Modern website design
Bright colours
– funky, youthful
look

4

Build consideration
by direct emailing
campaign
Develop retention
with special offers

17.2 Match the examples (1–4) with the summaries (a–d). Look at C opposite to help you.

1 Apple invented the iPod. They started to market it.
2 After a successful launch, Google got more and more market share.
3 Coca-Cola created new products (Diet Coke, BlaK, etc.) using the same brand.
4 Beaner's coffee changed the company name to Biggby Coffee at the beginning of 2008.
  The new name appears on signs and marketing material.

a They rebranded.
b The brand became established.
c They launched the brand.
d They stretched the brand.

17.3 Decide if the sentences below are true or false, and correct the false sentences. Look at A, B and C opposite to help you.

1 An advertising campaign is an example of brand values.
2 The brand strategy is a statement of the human characteristics of a brand.
3 Cinema advertising, packaging and website design are all examples of touchpoints.
4 You stretch a brand when you start communicating in a new advertising channel.
5 A brand that uses the same style in all its communications is doing total branding.
6 Brand management, brand vision and brand personality are all part of the brand platform.

17.4 Label the sections of the purchase funnel. Look at D opposite to help you.

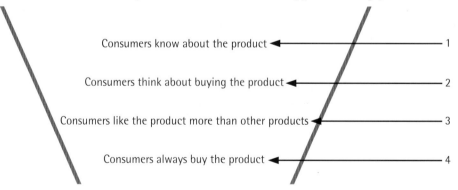

Consumers know about the product ← 1

Consumers think about buying the product ← 2

Consumers like the product more than other products ← 3

Consumers always buy the product ← 4

Over to you

An interesting theory is that you can brand people. Think of a politician or a famous person in your country. How would you advise this person on his / her brand platform? What changes would you suggest to the brand strategy?

18 Brand values

A Common brand values

Brand values are the code by which the brand lives and operates. They express how the brand wants to be seen by its consumers. Every brand has its own values, but there are some common brand values, which can be divided into subsets:

> Trust me.

A brand may be **respected** because it shows it is **knowledgeable about,** or has a very good **understanding of,** its **area of expertise** (for example, computing or finance) or its consumers. Many quality national newspapers have a **strong heritage** – they have built strong, lasting values over many years. They are **trustworthy** and **dependable** brands, often with an **international outlook** – reporting news from other countries. Some brands speak about their **trustworthiness** – their **integrity, honesty** and **responsibility** – and act in ways that are **fair** for the consumer and the environment. Other brands demonstrate their **leadership qualities** – the skills and knowledge to lead others. The Linux operating system and some open source software organizations allow consumers to contribute to their brand values: being **accessible, diverse, inclusive** and **independent.**

> I am good for you.

Customer satisfaction is key for brands that offer values like **great taste, low cost, value for money** or **good quality.** Brands speak about **flexibility, simplicity** and **practicality.** Being **easy to use** is a positive value. Some brands focus on a **healthy lifestyle** and are **nutritional, fresh** and **natural.** Some brands show they are **caring** and want to look after their consumers. A good example is the toy retailer Toys "R" Us, which includes **educational** as one of its values.

> I make you feel good.

Companies can use experiences and qualities as brand values:
discovery: the brand helps you discover or find out about things
pleasure: the brand gives you an enjoyable experience
passionate: the consumer and the brand share the same passions or strong feelings
inspirational: the brand can inspire the consumer to think about new things
vibrant or fun: the brand offers amusing experiences
active or dynamic: the brand is enthusiastic and has a lot of energy; it is constantly changing and adapting to the consumer
luxury: the brand promises high levels of comfort and beauty at a high price

> I am your contemporary.

Brands often mirror their consumers' values with their own. Young and modern brands will list in their brand values qualities like **modern, innovative, creative** and **technological.** More traditional brands will give their values as **classic, heritage, authentic** and **original.**

B Describing brand values

When describing brand values we can use both adjectives and nouns. We can say 'We are a modern and innovative brand' or 'Our values are modernity and innovation'.

For a list of adjectives and nouns to describe brand values, see Appendix IV on page 111.

18.1 Florette produce a range of ready-to-eat salads and salad dressings. Read what they say on their website about their brand values, and choose the correct heading from the box for each section. Look at A and B opposite and Appendix IV on page 111 to help you.

1 Educational	Dynamic	Freshness
2 International	Modernity	Value for money
3 Innovation	Naturalness	Honesty
4 Pleasure	Fun	Knowledgeable

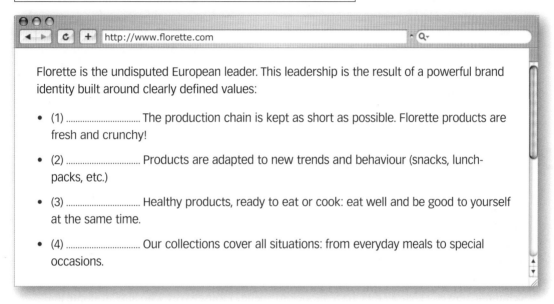

http://www.florette.com

Florette is the undisputed European leader. This leadership is the result of a powerful brand identity built around clearly defined values:

- (1) .... The production chain is kept as short as possible. Florette products are fresh and crunchy!

- (2) .... Products are adapted to new trends and behaviour (snacks, lunch-packs, etc.)

- (3) .... Healthy products, ready to eat or cook: eat well and be good to yourself at the same time.

- (4) .... Our collections cover all situations: from everyday meals to special occasions.

18.2 Choose the correct word from the brackets to complete each brand value statement. Look at A and B opposite to help you.

1 Our (trustworthiness / outlook / flexibility) means you can easily adapt the service to your needs.
2 We value (fresh / simplicity / inspirational) and we design our products with this in mind.
3 Our product is (easy to be / easy to use / easy to cost).
4 We are (knowledgeable / luxury / heritage) about food.
5 We are a low cost, value for (lifestyle / fun / money) brand.

18.3 Complete the brand value statements using words from the box. Look at A opposite to help you.

innovative	Inspirational	Luxury	Respected

1 Technology: we are .... and creative from product concept to packaging and delivery.
2 .... : we have a strong heritage in our area and we are knowledgeable.
3 .... : we value creativity, ours and yours. Together we build a more vibrant world.
4 .... : we believe that beautiful things have a high value and are worth the investment.

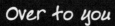

Over to you

Think about a brand you buy. What are the brand's values and how do they reflect your own values?

19 Market segmentation

A What is market segmentation?

Market segmentation identifies groups of buyers within a market who share similar needs and demonstrate similar purchasing behaviour. **Market segments** are described by **demographics** and **psychographics**.

Demographics

- **Age group** or **age bracket**: their age, for example 21–25
- **Sex**: **male / female split** – for example, 75% of *Elle* readers are women
- **Religion** or **ethnicity**: Hispanic, Asian, American, white, black, Muslim, Jewish, etc.
- **Income**: how much money a person earns; how **affluent**, or rich, they are
- **Life cycle**: single, married, with children

Psychographics

- **Education**: the highest qualification that a person has, such as a diploma or a degree
- **Attitudes** and **opinions**: how a person feels or thinks about issues, people, brands, etc.
- **Lifestyle**: a way of life that reflects a person's values and attitudes

B How does market segmentation work?

Demographics and psychographics are used to **target a segment** by using data to build up a **customer profile** – the image of a typical consumer. People can be targeted as individuals or as a family group that lives together and makes up a **household**. Marketers use the **ABC socio-economic categories** to target groups. In the UK this is known as **ACORN**, which stands for A Classification Of Residential Neighbourhoods. For a list of categories, see Appendix V on page 112.

ABs are a prized **customer segment**, as they have a **high disposable income** and **strong economic power** – that is, they have money to spend. **Housewives** who stay at home and look after the family are often the **main shoppers** for a household and are frequently targeted by marketers for certain types of products. Marketing messages that **appeal to singles** (unmarried people) will not be the same as the messages that appeal to the **specific tastes** of people **married with kids**. **City dwellers**, also known as **urbanites** – people who live in a city or a large **conurbation** or **metropolis** – will have different **preferences** from **country dwellers**. **Commuters** travel to their place of work from the country or suburbs and can be targeted on public transport or on out-of-home advertising along roadsides (see Unit 35).

> BrE: conurbation;
> AmE: metropolis

C Common market segments

Although every marketing department has its own definitions and names for the market segments they target, there are some common terms. In 1962 Everett Rogers described five market segments in his book *Diffusion of Innovations*:

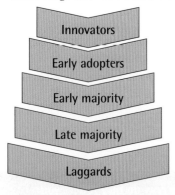

Innovators create something new and start a new trend.

Early adopters identify trends early and like to be associated with the start of a trend.

Early majority follow the trends set by the early adopters.

Late majority follow the trends that have been tested by the early majority.

Laggards are the last group of people to buy a product or brand: indeed they may never buy it.

Market segments may also be divided according to professions, lifestyles or age groups. For a list, see Appendix V on page 112.

19.1 Delete the incorrect word combination in each group. Then use the correct word combinations to complete the sentences below. Look at A, B and C opposite and Appendix V on page 112 to help you.

1	2	3	4
a customer segment	a early adopters	a market adopters	a married majority
b customer household	b early majority	b silver market	b late majority
c customer profile	c early market	c market segment	c early majority

1 .... like to try out new trends and products.
2 The .... is getting bigger as people live longer.
3 The .... try products that are well established in the marketplace.
4 Companies can build up a .... using market research.

19.2 Complete the text describing market segmentation for children's art supplies. Look at the page opposite and at Appendix V on page 112 to help you.

Kids' arts and crafts market growing

Kids' arts and crafts is brighter than ever, say many retailers. 'This (1) .... segment is growing without question. We're seeing a larger population of young kids entering school than in previous years and creating a great opportunity,' said Walgreens' spokesperson Yvette Anne Venable.

An increasing number of products are (2) .... at parents and grandparents who want their kids to be smart and creative, not just television junkies. Grandparents are a customer segment with strong economic (3) .... It is relatively easy to (4) .... to them using positive images of their grandchildren.

Steven Jacober, SHOPA's president, agrees: 'Art supplies and crafts continue to grow. This ties into the baby (5) .... generation, the way they are raising their children and their tendency to make everything a learning experience. There are a lot of different factors, and the demographics support continuing growth of the marketplace.'

Arts and crafts are targeted at households with (6) .... , kids aged 12 years and under.

19.3 Complete the descriptions (1–5) using words from the box. Then match the products with the market segments (a–e). Look at Appendix V on page 112 to help you.

affluent	appeal	income	life cycle	lifestyle

1 health insurance that covers the needs of people late in the ....
2 a hair care range for men with a modern .... and a self-indulgent attitude
3 a new TV channel broadcasting programmes that .... to homosexuals
4 a luxury range of executive stationery for an .... market segment
5 cheap to produce but fashionable sports shoes for a low .... segment

a gay and lesbian market	c teenagers	e C-level executives
b the silver market	d metrosexuals	

Over to you

Think about yourself. Which market segment(s) are you in? Is it the same for your friends and colleagues? List some products or brands that are targeted at you.

20 Customer needs and behaviour

A Maslow's Hierarchy of Needs

Abraham Maslow was a twentieth-century social psychologist. His pyramid of basic needs is one of the most cited models in marketing. Matt Robinson, a senior marketer for a high street bank, uses the model in a talk to the management team:

'Imagine that Mr Singh comes to see us about his pension plan. Of course, we talk about his **hopes and desires** for his retirement. We usually start with how to meet his **physiological needs**; by this we mean how he will pay for his food and housing – this is a **major customer concern**. We will also talk about **safety needs**, how our client will protect himself and his family when he is retired. We think about **social needs**: will he still be able to afford membership of the golf club? Then there is the Porsche that he drives to the golf club. This is an example of an **esteem need** – to **maintain** his lifestyle and social status. We talk a lot about golf in fact! There are also **self-fulfilment needs**: here we consider all Mr Singh's personal projects and dreams. We have to work out how much money he will need to invest today in order, for example, to be able to travel the world when he retires.'

Marketers are interested in **customer needs** as these can explain customer wants or desires for a specific product or service.

B Consumer Life Cycle (CLC)

Just as products have a life cycle, so do consumers – the **Consumer Life Cycle**, or **CLC**. Matt Robinson talks about this:

'Of course, the banking sector is highly **attuned to** consumer life cycles – we're able to understand how a customer's needs change over time. We exploit this by offering different services as our clients age, from their first savings account as a child, to a first current account, to mortgages, life insurance and retirement plans. Some people criticize us for **creating needs**, for making people believe they need products that they don't. But I really think we try to **fulfil**, or satisfy, customer needs as they change over the years. Younger customers do not have the same desires as retired people.'

C Purchasing behaviour

Purchasing behaviour or **purchasing patterns** refer to what a consumer buys, and when and how they make their **final purchasing decision**. The first step is usually awareness of the brand (see Unit 17). The consumer forms **purchase intentions** – plans to buy things – which they may or may not act on. **Routine purchases** of the same products on a repetitive basis (for example, coffee from the coffee machine at the office) have low levels of **personal involvement**. Major investments (such as buying a car) or **impulse purchasing** (such as buying some new shoes or a CD on the way home) have higher levels of personal involvement. Some consumers have very high levels of **loyalty** to a brand or product and they will always buy the same brand.

20.1 Match the needs from Maslow's pyramid (1–5) with the reasons for buying certain products (a–e). Look at A opposite to help you.

1 physiological needs
2 safety needs
3 social needs
4 esteem needs
5 self-fulfilment needs

a A consumer buys a smoke alarm for her house because she wants to be warned if there is a fire.
b A consumer buys a yearly subscription to a swimming pool because she would like to train and win a gold medal at the next Olympic Games.
c A consumer buys popcorn and drinks because he has invited his friends round to watch an important football match on the television.
d A consumer buys a chocolate bar because he is hungry.
e A consumer buys the latest fashion accessory so that she can look and feel good.

20.2 Correct the mistakes using words and expressions from A and B opposite.

1 Customers like to maintain a certain style for life.
2 A major customer's concern is how to provide for the immediate family.
3 Buying food and drink is an example of satisfying a physiological lifestyle.
4 Some service sectors are highly attuned with customer needs.
5 The Consumer Cycle shows how consumer needs change over a period of time.

20.3 A marketing specialist is talking about purchasing behaviour. Replace the underlined expressions with alternative expressions from C opposite. One question has two possible answers.

> The (1) actual decision to buy a product depends on the type of product or service. With yoghurt, for example, many customers wait until they are in the supermarket, in front of the row of yoghurts, before they decide. On the other hand, for a more expensive product, with higher (2) thought and psychological investment from the consumer, it may take place a long time before the purchase. Our research shows that some customers spend three years thinking about the next type of car they will buy. Obviously, over these three years the (3) plans to buy may change a lot. Then there are those (4) purchases without any thought because they are a habit that we all make without thinking. I always get pasta, eggs and milk at the supermarket so I never write them on the list and I always look out for special offers and promotions. This kind of (5) shopping habit is very difficult for a marketing team to change. However, (6) buying something you like when you see it is created by different customer needs, and here we can really make a difference.

1 ....   4 ....
2 ....   5 ....
3 ....   6 ....

Over to you

Think about some products you have bought recently and plot them on the line below.

high involvement   low involvement

◄───►

What kinds of needs were you satisfying with each purchase?

21 Loyalty programmes

A Customer loyalty

Customer loyalty is critical to business success and profitability. **Loyal customers** buy more, and so improve sales and profit margins. However, customers are becoming increasingly **fickle** or **disloyal** – they no longer hesitate to **switch**, or change, retailers and brands.

loyal /ˈlɔɪ.əl/ *adjective* firm and not changing in your support for a person, a company, an organization or a brand

,**customer 'loyalty** *noun* [U] the tendency to **repurchase** a particular product, service or brand, or **revisit** a particular company, shop or website

B Loyalty programmes

Marketers **implement loyalty programmes**, such as frequent flyer programmes, to **maximize customer loyalty** and to **minimize customer defection**. The purpose of a loyalty programme is to allow marketers to **identify** and **retain**, or keep, **preferred customers** and to **reward** them **with discounts** and **special offers**.

Most supermarkets and department stores have a **retail loyalty programme** in the form of a **store card** or **loyalty card**. Customers **complete** an **application form** with demographic data and receive a plastic card which is used firstly to **record information** about what the customer buys on their **transaction record**, and secondly to reward them with **vouchers, points** or **coupons,** which can all be used, or **redeemed,** to get gifts or money off future purchases.

BrE: loyalty programme; AmE: loyalty program

Note: A loyalty card can also be called a **rewards card**, a **points card**, or a **club card**.
Loyalty programmes are also known as **loyalty schemes**.

C Talking about loyalty programmes

Loyalty programmes are an effective tool to **build relationships** with customers.

Our loyalty card is suffering from **fatigue**. I mean, it's just one more card fighting for **wallet space**.

We operate an '**earn and burn**' scheme with our credit card. Customers **earn points** each time they pay with their card and **burn** them when they choose a **redemption option** from our catalogue — for example, a gift or a discount.

E-loyalty, a marketing company, has signed up several new partners for its **online loyalty programme**. Each company will use E-loyalty to **reward purchases** with **e-vouchers** that can be used online.

21.1 Choose the correct words from the brackets to complete the sentences. Look at A, B and C opposite to help you.

1 Market research shows that a satisfied customer does not automatically become a (loyalty / loyal) customer.
2 All retailers want customers to (repurchase / reward).
3 Loyalty programmes (reward / revisit) preferred customers.
4 Loyalty cards should maximize customer (defection / loyalty).
5 Customers (earn / burn) points when they pay using their credit card.
6 A great number of retailers (identify / implement) loyalty programmes.
7 (Transaction records / Special offers) track what customers buy.
8 To get a loyalty card, customers complete the (application form / demographic data).
9 Customers can (redeem / reward) their points at any of our partner stores.
10 Electronic goods are popular (reward purchases / redemption options).

21.2 Complete the newspaper article using words and expressions from the box. Look at A, B and C opposite to help you.

build	earn	preferred	retain
card	points	programmes	special offers

How loyal can you be?

Remember the first time you got a loyalty (1) .... from a retail store? You must have been on top of the world to be treated as a (2) .... customer. You looked for opportunities to shop only in that particular store to redeem your (3) .... and take advantage of discounts and (4) ....

With customer relationship management (CRM) becoming the buzzword of Indian industry, loyalty programmes are considered an effective tool to (5) .... relationships with customers across categories.

While loyalty (6) .... are popular among retail stores, the trend which is catching up is mall loyalty programmes. Ansal Plaza is among the first few Indian malls to offer a loyalty programme. Called the Ansal Plaza Privileges Program, it has more than 18 stores as programme partners. The programme enables the members to (7) .... and spend privilege points at any of these stores. It is a cost-efficient and cost-effective way for the programme partners to (8) .... customers. A stand-alone loyalty programme would need huge investments.

Over to you

Open your wallet or purse. How many loyalty cards are you carrying? What advantages do these cards give you?

22 Motivation marketing

What is motivation marketing?

For most organizations, staff are the **key to success** – the most important tool for the organization's success – and they can be **motivated** to promote their company's product or service. **Motivation marketing** engages staff and gets them interested by using **events** or **incentives** (see below). It also aims to **recognize** and **reward staff efforts** by offering prizes or **rewards** for good performance – for example, with a **monthly incentive**.

Other benefits of motivation marketing include:

- **increased job satisfaction:** happier people at work
- **improved productivity:** more work done in less time
- **improved performance:** the work is done better
- **encouraging behaviour changes:** for example, introducing new work practices
- **increased sales force effectiveness:** for example, to achieve higher sales figures
- **improved product launches: boost market penetration** and gain market share more quickly.

Staff incentive schemes

Staff incentive schemes, also known as **incentive programmes** – formal schemes designed to encourage staff to act in a certain way – are used by a wide range of companies in order to improve staff and distributor performance. Incentives such as prizes, rewards or gifts can **boost morale** (make staff feel more positive about their job and their employer). **Building staff loyalty** will result in lower **staff turnover** or **churn** – that is, fewer people leaving the company. Another benefit is **reduced staff absenteeism**, a reduction in the number of days when employees are not at work through sickness. Measuring **staff reaction** and **getting feedback** – finding out what staff think about the programme – are essential to getting it right.

Ipoints, a company that runs trade and staff incentive programmes, developed a prize-winning staff loyalty programme for Healthcare Staffers, an agency that places temporary medical staff in clinics and hospitals.

Best Staff Loyalty Programme

WINNER: VIPpoints, developed for HealthCare Staffers

Healthcare Staffers **wanted to attract and retain temporary medical staff** for placement in hospitals.

The agency developed VIPpoints. A **welcome pack** (containing valuable information for new members) and **membership card** (used to identify the worker and to **collect points**) were sent to temporary medical staff. Members **earned points** every time they worked for Healthcare Staffers.

Healthcare Staffers' **internal staff** were also **included in the points scheme** and could also choose rewards from the **points catalogue**.

Note: **Loyalty schemes** are used to motivate customers – see Unit 21.

Incentives: travel and events

In order to motivate staff, a company may choose to use **cash substitutes** or **noncash awards** such as a travel incentive – sending staff on a short trip or holiday.

Big ticket giveaways, such as cars or very expensive holidays, are effective **sales incentives** – they can help motivate staff to sell more. During the **qualifying period** for an award or prize, teams are usually more motivated. **Nominations** for awards can come from colleagues. Sometimes an employee may be **nominated** by a manager, perhaps because of high sales figures.

Events, such as parties, weekends away, games and competitions, can be very successful for **team building** – increasing effective **teamwork** within a company or department.

22.1 Complete the sentences using words from the box. Look at A, B and C opposite to help you.

build	internal	reaction	recognizing	sales	turnover

1 Motivation marketing is a good way to .... staff loyalty.
2 It can increase motivation levels by .... staff efforts.
3 A good incentive scheme means that people want to stay with the company, there is lower staff ....
4 Travel is an effective .... incentive.
5 People working inside the company, the .... staff, benefit from incentive schemes.
6 A good incentive scheme measures staff .... to make sure everything is going well.

22.2 The following lines (1–6) are from an article about incentive programmes. Put them in the correct order, then say if the sentences (a–c) below are true or false. Look at B opposite to help you.

1 and flowers. Up For It! reinforces the agency's dynamic culture. Staff
2 incentive for individuals and teams which rewards and
3 The programme, Up For It!, was launched at the start of last year. There is a monthly
4 absenteeism decreased significantly during the year.
5 recognizes those who represent the company's values. Employees can be nominated
6 by colleagues for rewards including perfume, free parking at the office,

a Absenteeism went up while the incentive scheme was running.
b Points were awarded to staff.
c Employees cannot nominate themselves for rewards.

22.3 Complete the descriptions of incentive schemes using words from the box. Look at A, B and C opposite to help you.

collected	encourage	membership	scheme
earned	force	qualifying	welcome

1 Incentivise is a knowledge-based staff training and incentive .... that rewards staff for learning. Every member of staff receives a .... card and a .... pack. When enough points have been .... , staff can exchange their points for gifts.
2 A large employer is concerned when absenteeism climbs above the national average. The company launches an incentive scheme to .... behaviour changes. All employees who have taken no days off each quarter are entered into a draw to win prizes, including holidays. During the .... period staff attendance rose dramatically.
3 The Australian Tourist Commission has launched an incentive scheme to increase sales .... effectiveness. Sales staff who sell a luxury holiday can enter to win a new car. Initial reactions suggest that it will really help to energize the team and make them more dynamic.

Over to you

Think about an organization or company you know well. What kind of team building event would work best for the staff? Prepare some notes to present your idea to the head of the company.

23 Customer Relationship Management

A One-to-one marketing

Don Peppers, a marketing guru, answers questions in an online interview.

> What is **one-to-one marketing**, and how does it differ from traditional marketing?

Don Peppers, the one-to-one marketing guru

'In a nutshell, one-to-one marketing, also known as **Customer Relationship Management** or **CRM**, is based on the idea of treating different customers differently. Companies in all industries today are faced with the double problems of declining customer loyalty and shrinking profit margins. One-to-one marketing strategies enable companies to **create long-term, mutually beneficial relationships with customers**. These result in greater customer loyalty and improved margins.'

> What are some steps a company could take to **implement one-to-one marketing** effectively?

'One-to-one organizations create a **customer feedback loop** in which they say, 'I know you. You tell me what you want. I'll make it – and I'll remember next time.' We call this process a **learning relationship**, and it has four basic implementation steps (IDIC):

- **IDENTIFY your customers** at all points of contact.
- **DIFFERENTIATE between** your customers based on their individual needs and value to your organization.
- **INTERACT** with your customers in a **two-way dialogue**.
- **CUSTOMIZE** or **TAILOR** some aspect of your products or services based on what you learn from your customers.'

B CRM technology

CRM technology supports a CRM strategy by **gathering, storing** and **analysing customer data**. **Front office systems,** such as call centres or loyalty cards (see Unit 21), gather information directly from clients, which is then **stored** and **processed** in a **back office system** called a **database** or **data warehouse**. (A data warehouse contains information from different databases.) Back office systems make it possible for a company to follow sales and fulfill orders.

The marketing department can use software tools to **mine the data** (analyse the data) stored in the data warehouse. **Data mining reveals patterns** in customer behaviour. For example, fathers have a tendency to buy branded food products, whilst mothers prefer private labels (see Unit 16). Relationship marketers can then **tailor** or **customize their marketing efforts** towards the customer. With CRM technology, **mass customization** is possible. This means that each customer will receive slightly different offers and discounts.

C Privacy

Consumer protection groups or **watchdogs** are concerned about the gathering and storing of large quantities of customer information. A company should **protect** its customers' **privacy**. Customers may wish to keep their purchases **confidential,** or secret. Most companies have a **privacy policy**. They promise not to **disclose customer data** by revealing it to other people, or to **share customer records** with other companies. Companies **encrypt the information,** changing it into a secret code. This ensures that it is not available to people outside the company, and so prevents accidental **disclosure of information**.

Note: To find out more about privacy laws in the UK, search online for information about the Data Protection Act.

23.1 Find verbs and prepositions in A, B and C opposite that can be used to make word combinations from the opposite page with the nouns below.

....
....   (**customers**)   ....
....
                                                                               ....   (**data**)
                                                                               ....
                                                                               ....
                                                                               ....

23.2 Complete the sentences using word combinations from 23.1 above. Then decide if the statements were made by CRM marketers, consumers, or representatives of a consumer watchdog.

1 Our privacy policy guarantees that we will not .... data or share customer records with other companies.
2 Purchasing records can be used against consumers. In one recent divorce case a woman used the data .... when her husband used a loyalty card to prove he had a high income.
3 I like to receive discounts and vouchers. To be honest, I don't mind if someone .... data on how much coffee and tea I buy.
4 We can, for example, ... between customers who have small children and those with teenagers.

23.3 Patricia Clement is in charge of CRM for an online cosmetics boutique. She is explaining their marketing strategy to potential investors. Choose the correct words from the brackets to complete the presentation. Look at A and B opposite to help you.

'... At BigChoiceCosmetics.com, we believe that customer loyalty is key. We concentrate on building long-term (1) .... (needs / relationships / feedback loops) with our customers.

How do we do it? Like many successful dotcom companies, we have implemented a one-to-one or (2) .... (CRM / data warehousing / data mining) approach. The first step is to (3) .... (gather / identify / analyse) our customers – before buying cosmetics from our website, customers register their personal details and preferences. We (4) .... (differentiate / store / customize) this information in a (5) .... (database / front office system / watchdog) so the next time the customer visits, we know who they are. Over time we build up a customer (6) .... (value / record / pattern). We can (7) .... (differentiate / customize / implement) between our customers based on their needs – what they buy, and on their value – how much they spend.

People often ask me about our communication strategy. At BigChoiceCosmetics.com we prefer to talk about (8) .... (learning / interacting / treating) with our customers in a two-way (9) .... (loop / data warehouse / dialogue). Let me give you an example. Last year we launched an e-magazine called the BigChoiceCosmetics Guide. We emailed over 500 versions of the Guide! This is what the CRM expert, Don Peppers, calls mass (10) .... (customization / marketing / data mining). Take, for instance, Miss Brown: she is 17, and recently bought lipstick from our Fashion range. She received articles about top models and a competition to win free samples of a new lipstick. We didn't send her discount vouchers for anti-ageing cream, but we did send them to her grandmother!

As I said, we have (11) .... (gathered / tailored / revealed) a huge amount of information. Today, our major challenge is to exploit the data stored in our (12) .... (database / pattern / front office system). We need your help to invest in sophisticated (13) .... (data mining / learning / relationship) software ...'

Over to you

Find three offers that you have received from companies by email or post. Were these offers tailored to you? If so, how did the company obtain your personal information?

24 The marketing budget

A The marketing budget

Marketing must contribute to the **profitability** of a business – how much profit it makes. The **marketing budget** presents the cost of the marketing plan (see Unit 4). It can include the cost of distribution and different **marketing actions**, such as advertising or market research. The **annual marketing budget** shows what the marketing department is planning to spend over the year. Management may ask the marketing team to **justify** or **modify the budget** before **giving approval**.

B Budgeting approaches

There are several approaches to **setting the marketing budget** – that is, fixing spending on **marketing** – for example, investment in research or advertising:

- the **affordable approach**
  The company **forecasts revenues** (predicts the amount of money it expects from sales), deducts costs, and **allocates** a part of the remaining funds to promotion. Marketing is considered as a cost that can be **cut** (reduced), depending on what the company can **afford** – that is, how much money it has left.

- the **percentage of sales approach**
  A percentage of current or **anticipated sales** (what a company expects to sell) is **allocated** to marketing actions. Typically, ten **percent of net sales** is spent on promotion.

- the **objective-and-task approach**
  The company **costs out**, or calculates, the cost of reaching its **marketing objectives**. For example, new products will need large advertising budgets to build awareness.

- **competitive parity**
  Competitor investment is **tracked**, or monitored, and used as a **rule of thumb** (a guideline) to set the promotion budget. The objective is to **beat** (spend more than) or **match** (spend the same as) the investment of competitors.

Whichever approach is chosen, marketers need to **respect the budget** – that is, not **go over budget** (spend more than planned) or **be under budget** (invest less than planned).

Note: Another way of saying **respect the budget** is **be on budget**. For information on language for presenting a budget, see Unit 9 and Appendix III on page 110.

C Return on investment (ROI)

Marketers are **accountable for** – that is, responsible for – their budget. They must demonstrate that their marketing actions are **cost-effective** (productive relative to the cost) and not a **waste of money**.

> Half the money I **spend on advertising** is **wasted**; the trouble is I don't know which half.

John Wanamaker, 19th century American department store owner

The marketing plan establishes how to measure the **return on investment** (**ROI**) or the **cost-effectiveness** of different marketing actions – the amount of profit made based on the amount of resources needed to make it. **Monthly**, **quarterly** and **annual reviews** of **performance against budget** measure **projected**, or forecast, results against **real performance** – how the company actually performed. Many companies use statistics called **marketing metrics** to **quantify** the performance of their marketing activities. They can include items such as market share, advertising spend or response rates for direct marketing.

To talk about the cost-effectiveness of marketing actions, marketers say:

If we analyse the **cost per**	lead, client, response,	we can see that this	is a / isn't a	**cost-effective**	way of spending our marketing budget.

24.1 Match the two parts of the sentences. Look at A and B opposite to help you.

1 Marketing should contribute   a justify the marketing budget.
2 The marketing budget sets   b the budget.
3 The marketing director may need to   c competitor spending.
4 Companies track   d to the profitability of a firm.
5 Marketers should respect   e out the cost of the marketing plan.

24.2 Complete the postings from a marketing website using words from the box. Then say which budgeting approaches are mentioned in the posts. Look at B opposite to help you.

afford	cost	match	percent	setting	thumb
allocate	cut	objectives	respect	task	

---

(1) .... **a Marketing Budget**

Posted By Khouse:

Are there any rules of (2) .... for setting a marketing budget?

Posted by ChamberE

I suggest using a mix of objective-and- (3) .... and affordability methods. Decide on your marketing (4) .... Then determine and (5) .... out the marketing tactics you need to implement. Finally, compare those costs with what you can (6) .... to spend. You have to (7) .... your budget. If you are over budget, you will need to (8) .... costs.

Posted by MattAp

It depends on what your competitors are spending. You need to (9) .... the spending of the market leader.

Posted by CathE

There are guidelines by industry. What industry are you servicing? Many companies (10) .... a percentage of expected sales to marketing support. High tech companies can spend up to fifty (11) .... of net sales on promotion.

Posted By Khouse:

Thanks to you all for your responses. I can see it depends a lot on the type of business and its objectives. Thanks again – I appreciate your help.

Over to you

Imagine that you are preparing a marketing budget for a non-profit organization. Explain the different possible approaches to setting the marketing budget to the organization's members.

25 Price

A Pricing strategies

Marketing Teacher is a website for marketing students. The following extract looks at some strategies to consider when **fixing a price**.

Premium pricing: Use a high price where there is a substantial competitive advantage – for example, rooms in Savoy hotels.

Penetration pricing: The price charged for products and services is set artificially low in order to gain market share. Once this is achieved, the price is increased.

Economy pricing: Marketing and manufacturing costs are kept to a minimum. Supermarkets often have economy brands for soups, spaghetti, etc.

Price skimming: Charge a high price because you have a new product type. However, the high price attracts new competitors into the market, and the price falls due to increased supply. DVD players were launched with this strategy.

Psychological pricing: The consumer responds on an emotional, rather than rational, basis. For example, charging 99 cents instead of 1 dollar.

Captive product pricing: Companies will charge a premium price where the consumer cannot choose a competitive product.

Product bundle pricing: Sellers combine several products in the same package. This also serves to move old stock. Videos and CDs are often sold using the bundle approach.

B Pricing considerations

The marketing team for Stick Tea are preparing for a meeting about the price of a new range of tea that comes in a stick instead of a bag. They make notes on **pricing considerations**.

* <u>Alternative solutions</u>: our stick packaging is unique
* <u>Ease of comparison</u>: easy to compare price but difficult to compare taste
* <u>Unique benefits / Unique Selling Points (USPs)</u>: quality of tea; stick format
* <u>Monetary significance</u>: tea is cheap, but the innovative packaging has a <u>high value</u>
* <u>Demand</u>: tea consumption is stable, but sales in speciality shops are on the rise
* <u>Price sensitivity</u>: consumers are very <u>price sensitive</u> - sales decrease when prices increase
* <u>Complementary costs</u>: none - the customer doesn't even need a spoon!!

C The price test

Stick Tea decide to carry out a **price test** for their range of tea. They want to know what customers think is a **fair price** for a box of 50 sticks. They are also interested in comparing different possible retail **price points** (€12, €14 and €16), to find out what customers consider to be the **full price** and the **bargain price** for a box of 250 sticks.

25.1 Read the descriptions and name the pricing strategies that are being used. Look at A opposite to help you.

1 charging a high amount for bottles of water inside a football stadium during the World Cup
2 charging $2.95 instead of $3
3 charging a low price to win sales in a new market
4 packaging shampoo, conditioner and hair gel from the same hair care product line together, and charging one price for the lot

25.2 Match the questions about pricing strategy (1–7) to the pricing considerations (a–g). Look at B opposite to help you.

1 What is the value of the product or service for the consumer?
2 What is special or different about the product or service?
3 Is it difficult to compare the price and quality of similar products or services?
4 How many people want to buy the product or service?
5 How many similar products or services are there on the market?
6 What else does the consumer need to pay for in order to use the product or service?
7 How much does a change in price affect consumer demand for the product or service?

a alternative solutions
b ease of comparison
c unique benefits
d monetary significance
e demand
f price sensitivity
g complementary costs

25.3 Complete the text using words from the box. Look at A, B and C opposite to help you.

bargain	fair	premium	significance	unique
costs	points	sensitive	solutions	

When deciding on the price of a product or service you have to consider the product or service itself. For example, does it have (1) .... benefits? Does the consumer have any alternative (2) .... ? What is the monetary (3) .... of the product or service? You also have to think about the possibility of complementary (4) .... , and how price (5) .... the consumers are to these and the product or the service cost.

Then you need to think about the pricing strategy and how this relates to the brand. For a luxury brand it is essential to follow a (6) .... pricing strategy in order to maintain the brand image. A no-frills low price would not be suitable for a brand such as Cartier.

Finally, you need to carry out a price test to check the price (7) .... you are considering. The (8) .... price is the amount that the consumer is prepared to pay for the product or service. A (9) .... price is a low price that may be used during special offers or for promotional pricing.

Over to you

Think about three products you have bought recently. Identify the pricing strategy.

26 Logistics and the distribution chain

A Moving goods

Logistics is the management of the transport and storage of goods. Marcus Bridgestone, the logistics manager for a plastic packaging company, is talking to a new assistant about the **distribution chain**.

Marcus: After completion, items get sent from the factory to the **warehouse**. We store them there until we are ready to **ship**, or deliver, to the client. I say 'ship' but we don't always use a boat to do it. The cheapest, but slowest, **shipping method** is by **container ship**, but it takes around five weeks to sail from Asia to Europe. Sometimes we need to move the **shipments** or **freight** much faster, so we use **air freight**. However, it's much more expensive, although it depends on the weight of the **load** – the goods being carried. When the shipment gets to Europe we have a number of **shipping options**, which really depend on where the goods **land** – I mean, where they arrive – and where we have to deliver them. **Rail freight** is cheap but not always reliable, depending on the country. **Road haulage** is more expensive but the advantage is that lorries can go right up to the doors of shops or factories.

Assistant: What about the man from the **delivery service**?

Marcus: George, from Fedex? We try only to use delivery services when we need to send something small, or very urgently.

> BrE: lorry; AmE: truck

B Direct distribution

This website extract describes how Dell, the computer manufacturer, distributes its products:

```
⊖ ○ ○
```

Michael Dell started Dell Computers in 1984 with only $1,000. Dell has grown to be a company with average daily earnings of $40 million. How did he do it? A new concept: **eliminate the middlemen** and **sell directly** to the consumer. Dell has been able to maintain complete control over stock levels – that is, how much stock it holds at any one time – as well as **distribution costs**.

Dell figured out a new way to sell computers to the consumer, which was through **direct distribution**. Dell was able to gain a competitive advantage for several reasons:

- First of all, direct distribution allows Dell to **eliminate wholesalers**, who buy and sell goods in large amounts to shops and businesses. This is an advantage because Dell does not have to deal with wholesalers or spend time **keeping track of inventory** in the wholesalers' warehouses – that is, monitoring what the wholesaler has in stock.

- Secondly, Dell has **eliminated retailers** – the people, shops or businesses that sell to the public. This is effective because Dell does not have to **receive customer orders** from thousands of different retailers. It can take orders directly from the customer.

Note: **Stock** or **inventory**? See Appendix I on page 108.

C Indirect distribution

Unlike Dell, most manufacturers or **service providers** use an **indirect distribution channel** to **connect** the product and the consumer, where some kind of **distributor** or **distribution intermediary** is used. For illustrations and descriptions of intermediaries see Appendix VI on page 113.

26.1 Label the parts of the distribution chain using words from the box. Look at A opposite to help you.

air freight	delivery service	rail freight	warehouse
container ship	a load	road haulage	

1

2

3

4

5

6

7

26.2 Put the steps in the distribution chain in the correct order. Look at A and C opposite to help you.

1 The goods arrive and can be sold to the consumer.
2 The franchise sends the order to the warehouse in South America.
3 Road haulage is used to ship the goods from Southampton to Brighton.
4 The goods land in Southampton.
5 The container ship is loaded with the parts.
6 A franchisee in Brighton places an order for car accessories.

26.3 Find six words from A, B and C opposite that can be used to make word combinations with *distribution*. Then use some of the combinations to complete the cost controller's report.

....
....

(distribution)

....
....
....
....

(1) .... were very high last year so this year we have advised all project managers to use air freight as little as possible. Another possible source of high costs has been the length of the (2) .... for our product. Although we have been trying to develop (3) .... by attracting more customers to our website and encouraging them to order from us, most of our products get to market through an (4) .... channel. We have been seeking ways to cut down the number of wholesalers and other types of (5) .... We are beginning to deal directly with retailers and in the long run this will reduce our costs.

Over to you
What distribution channels can farmers use for their products?

27 Merchandising

A Merchandise and merchandising

Merchandising is used to describe a marketing practice in which the brand image of one product, the **core brand**, is used to sell another product. For example, a famous character such as Mickey Mouse is used to sell Disney **merchandise** such as bags and clothes. The goal is to **increase retail sales**.

Note: The noun **merchandising** is also used by the retail sector to describe a range of activities designed to promote in-store sales, including supermarket listings (see Unit 15) and POS (see Unit 41).

B Promotional merchandise

Gifts with purchase can increase sales. Examples include:

- **in-pack offers** – items inside the packaging, such as a toy in a box of breakfast cereal
- **on-pack offers** – gifts, including money-off offers and competitions, which are promoted on the packaging and can be obtained by following the instructions given.

Other types of **promotional gift** include:

- **freebies** or **goodies** – promotional items which are given away, such as free perfume samples or sun hats with the company logo
- **corporate gifts** – luxury items with a company logo, given to special clients or VIPs.

An international merchandising company, Event Merchandising, discusses how to select promotional gifts:

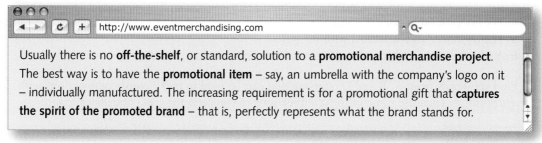

http://www.eventmerchandising.com

Usually there is no **off-the-shelf**, or standard, solution to a **promotional merchandise project**. The best way is to have the **promotional item** – say, an umbrella with the company's logo on it – individually manufactured. The increasing requirement is for a promotional gift that **captures the spirit of the promoted brand** – that is, perfectly represents what the brand stands for.

C Sports merchandising

Sports clubs can develop additional revenues by selling **team products,** such as shirts and memorabilia, at a premium price. They can also sign **merchandising deals** or **licensing deals** with **sponsors** or other **commercial partners** (see Unit 48 on sponsorship). The club authorizes, or **licenses**, the partner to use the club's logo on their products. For example, Lego bought the right to use the NBA league logo on their figurines.

D Film, book and music merchandising

Merchandising is often used in the promotion of films, books, bands and pop stars. This extract is from an article about the marketing of Harry Potter products:

Harry Potter has become a marketing and merchandising phenomenon with **spin-offs** and **tie-ins** in the shape of games, figurines, clothing and even food. Hundreds of millions of dollars have been agreed in **licensing deals** – the right for another company to use the Harry Potter characters on their merchandise. This is known as **cross-marketing**, as the sale of Harry Potter merchandise helps promote the Harry Potter books, and vice versa.

27.1 Choose the correct words from the brackets to complete the report on Bob the Builder merchandising. Look at A, B and D opposite to help you.

Bob the Builder's enormous financial success is due only in part to the TV programme. The (1) .... (merchant / deal / core brand) has been used to create pyjamas, party hats and plates. It's important to create something that will sell (2) .... (core brands / corporate gifts / merchandise) that parents are happy to buy. Bob the Builder items have also been used as promotional (3) .... (gifts / successes / brands) in connection with other brands. This type of (4) .... (spin-offs / sponsors / cross-marketing) has generated profit for all the brands involved.

27.2 Put the descriptions (1–3) in the correct order and then match them to the pictures (a–c). Look at B opposite to help you.

1

| offer really captures the | brand. | This on-pack | spirit of the promoted |

2

| gift is ideal for | pack. This kind of promotional | children. | There is a small freebie inside the |

3

| solution for your corporate | These promotional | gifts. | items are an off-the-shelf |

27.3 Make word combinations using words from the box. Then use the word combinations to complete the text below. Look at B, C and D opposite to help you.

| commercial | deals | licensing | partners | products | team |

David Beckham started his career as a footballer. He has signed (1) .... all over the world and has made a fortune for himself and his (2) .... When he started playing for Real Madrid, sales of (3) .... such as football shirts rose rapidly.

Over to you

Think of a popular personality or character (film star, pop star, children's character, sports personality, etc.). What kind of merchandising would or would not be appropriate for them? Give reasons for your choices.

28 Trade shows

A Why use trade shows?

A **trade show**, **trade exhibition** or **trade fair** is an industry-specific **business event**. Companies **attend** the events so that they can **showcase**, or display, the best of their products, services or expertise. Trade shows help to **generate leads** (create opportunities for future business) and can offer great opportunities to **network** – to chat and socialize with **attendees** (people visiting the show) and other **exhibitors**.

A **public trade show** is open to everyone. If the trade show is only open to people who work in a specific business sector, it is referred to as **trade only**. A **vertical trade show** specializes in everything for a specific sector – for example, cosmetics, which will showcase fragrances, packaging, etc. A **horizontal trade show** is for a certain industry. For a packaging fair this might include cardboard manufacturers, vac form producers, etc. (See Unit 45)

A stand at a trade show

Seminars, **conferences** or **congresses** are business events where talks or presentations are given. The **organizers** are often medical or pharmaceutical companies.

Note: Trade show, trade exhibition or trade fair? Seminar, conference or congress? See Appendix I on page 108.

B Organizing an event

Helen Jackson works for a conference centre in the UK that **hosts** many international fairs. She gives advice to potential exhibitors on her website:

Make your **stand** or **booth** a marketing success by using this checklist:

- Find out about the **event profile** and how successful previous years have been. Most importantly, check that the **visitor profile** matches your audience.

- If you decide to **participate in the event**, **book a stand**. Most organizers **allocate stand placement** on a 'first come first served' basis. Calculate the **floor space** you need. Remember that bigger stands cost more.

- Prepare your booth and customize it with **trade show displays**. A good booth design will **increase booth traffic** and attract more visitors.

- Train **booth staffers**. Make sure the people who are representing your company and your brand know how to win clients. This human contact is crucial for **maintaining** or **improving current client perception** – that is, what your customers think about your brand.

- Make sure your visitors know how to get to the **venue**. Download the colour map from our site.

- Please remember that nobody likes **lobbysquatters** sitting in the entrance to the venue. If you are coming to our venue, please use a stand. **Lobbysquatting** is not tolerated and you will be asked to leave.

Note: The nouns **booth** and **stand** are interchangeable.
For more information on **trade show displays**, see Unit 41.

28.1 Make word combinations with *trade show* using words from A and B opposite. Then use the combinations to complete the sentences below.

....
....
....

(**trade show**)

....

1 I think we should try to interact directly with our customers. We should find out about a
.... that anyone can go to.
2 You mean a .... that has everything for the house and home decoration?
3 Yes, like the Home and House Show. But it looks expensive. We'll have to reuse the
.... from last year.
4 OK, and how about a .... where we can meet other people in the candle-making sector? Last year's Candle-makers' Fair was very useful.

28.2 Make word combinations using a word or phrase from each box. One phrase can be used twice. Look at A and B opposite to help you.

allocate	trade shows
attend	stand placement
book	booth traffic
increase	a stand
participate in	

28.3 Complete the article using words from the box. Then decide if the statements (a–c) below are true or false. Look at A and B opposite to help you.

| network | seminars | showcase | stands | trade | venue |

---

http://www.wineinstitute.org

The Wine Institute organizes wine (1) .... shows and conducts educational (2) .... and visitor programs to acquaint media and trade representatives with California wines. California vintners will (3) .... a record 128 California wine brands at the world's largest wine trade show.
The (4) .... for VINEXPO is always Bordeaux, France. VINEXPO attracts 50,000 buyers, industry trade representatives and journalists from 120 countries. In addition to preparing their own (5) .... , California vintners will sponsor a restaurant at VINEXPO: the California Grill. California wineries use the grill to (6) .... with important clients and show them California cuisine and California wines while conducting major business.

WINE INSTITUTE
THE VOICE FOR CALIFORNIA WINE

a Vinexpo is a relatively small public trade show.
b The event is a good place to meet buyers and journalists.
c Californian vintners don't have stands at this event.

Over to you

Select a product or service to promote. Which trade fair would you attend? Design your stand. Think about staffers, displays, etc.

29 Telemarketing

A What is telemarketing?

Telemarketing is a form of **direct marketing**: the messages are delivered individually to potential customers. It requires an **immediate response** – when the phone rings, the natural response is to answer it. It provides a company with **immediate feedback** – you can find out what a potential customer thinks straight away. It also provides a **captive audience** – the person who answers the phone usually stays to listen for a few minutes. The success of telemarketing campaigns is measured in the **cost per acquisition, cost per inquiry** (**CPI**) or **cost per order**.

B Outbound telemarketing

With **outbound telemarketing, telemarketers** (also known as **telemarketing operators**) call **prospects** (potential clients) from a list. Lists can be bought from **list brokers**. A **cold list** is a list of people who have had no prior contact with the company. Calling the people on the list for the first time is known as **cold calling**. A **qualified telemarketing list** includes the details about prospects who have the need or authority to purchase.

Common reasons for cold calling include:

- **lead generation** – contacting **cold prospects** (people who don't yet have a relationship with the company) to create **hot contacts** (people who are ready to buy)
- **phone sales** – selling services over the telephone
- **appointment setting** – making an appointment for a sales rep to meet the prospect.

Follow-up calls may take place after a mailshot (see Unit 42) or a trade show (see Unit 28). Telemarketers try to **convert** these leads into sales. This is called **lead conversion**.

Voice broadcasting is a cheaper form of outbound telemarketing. Instead of having a **live operator** – that is, an actual person – a **recorded message** is played to the prospect or left on their answering machine.

C Inbound telemarketing

With **inbound telemarketing**, clients call the telemarketing firm, perhaps in response to an advert, to **place an order**, **make a reservation** or **contact customer services**.

D Telemarketing scripts

Telemarketing operators are trained to **deal with objections** (reasons people give for not buying). **Telemarketing scripts** list the questions that must be asked and what must be said to reassure the potential client. Here is an example of a telemarketing script:

Good morning / afternoon. May I speak with Mr / Mrs Mandeville please?

My name is Julie. **I'm calling on behalf of** Paper Express. **Are you aware of the company at all?**

NO: That's OK. It's a mail order company that provides discounted paper and office supplies. (then to YES)

YES: **Are you the person in charge of purchasing office supplies?**

NO: **May I ask for the name of that person?** (take details)

YES: **The reason for my call is** to see whether you are interested in meeting one of our sales team.

NO: **Thank you for your time.** (end call)

YES: **Would you be available for a meeting on Friday morning?** (take details, end call)

29.1 Complete the crossword. Look at A, B, C and D
opposite to help you.

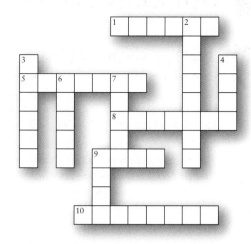

Across
1 After a mailshot we always make
.............................-up calls. (6)
5 Telemarketing provides a .... audience
for the sales team. (7)
8 Our .... telemarketing operators
handle calls from clients. (7)
9 We plan to use telemarketing for ....
generation. (4)
10 A .... message is cheaper than a live
operator. (8)

Down
2 .... telemarketing will help us to generate leads. (8)
3 We need to prepare the telemarketing .... carefully so that our team know exactly
what to say. (6)
4 By ....-calling we generated enough leads to keep us busy for months. (4)
6 In just two days we made a lot of .... sales. (5)
7 We decided to use .... broadcasting because it is much less expensive than having
a person there to make the call. (5)
9 You need to write a script for a .... operator. (4)

29.2 George House is the marketing manager of a local newspaper. Here are some extracts
from his presentation of a direct marketing campaign. Choose the correct words from the
brackets to complete the sentences. Look at A, B and D opposite to help you.

1 We decided to use (outbound / prospect) telemarketing.
2 We met our subscription target at an acceptable cost per (objection / acquisition).
3 Use (immediate / direct) marketing to increase the number of subscribers to the newspaper.
4 We bought a (qualified / captive) list from a (telemarketing / list) broker.
5 Telemarketing operators received special training to (contact / deal) with objections.
6 We created a new (script / conversion) with our telemarketing firm.

Now say if the sentences refer to the objective, the action plan or the results.

29.3 Correct the mistakes in the telemarketing script using words and expressions from D opposite.

1 Hello, my name is John. I'm calling of behalf on Jupiter Software.
2 Do you aware of the company at all?
3 Are you the person charged with this?
4 My call reason is to find out if you are interested in our latest products.
5 Do you available for an appointment?

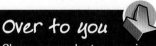

Over to you
Choose a product or service you would like to promote. Write a brief for a telemarketing firm.

30 | Online shopping and mail order

The online shopping experience

A **virtual shopkeeper** gives some advice:

'When designing an online store, you need to think about how to **move your shopper through the sales process**, getting them quickly and easily from your **home page**, where their shopping experience begins, through to the **checkout**, where they pay. You also have to think about ways to personalize the **selection process** – how people choose what to buy. Some visitors may **search by product category**, while others will want to **browse**, visiting the whole store just to see what there is. Some clients may want to create a **wish list** of the items they would like to receive as presents, or set up a **wedding list** or **baby registry** to let other people know what gifts they want if they're getting married or having a child. To attract clients to purchase, you can **offer bundles of items**. For example, an online sports store could sell tennis rackets and tennis balls together as a single item.

It's important to simplify the **purchasing process** – how customers pay for goods they are **ordering online**. It should be very easy for your clients to **add items to the shopping cart** or **shopping basket** when they've decided what they want to buy by clicking on the "**add to basket**" button or the "**buy now**" button. Once they are at the checkout you should give clear **payment information**, which must include details about **delivery costs** and **delivery options**. You may want to give your customers the choice of **next day delivery** at a premium price. You should also list the **payment options** for your customers, such as gift certificates, credit cards or cheques.'

> BrE: cheque; AmE: check

Mail order and the ordering process

Mail order is a system of buying and selling goods through the post. Customers normally select their goods from a catalogue. The instructions below tell customers how to order a product from a company's catalogue:

> Please complete the **order form** below and return it to us in the **prepaid envelope** provided – you don't need a stamp. Alternatively, you can call our **telephone hotline** and **place your order**. Calls are free on our **Freephone number**.

Item code	Size	Description	Quantity	Price each	Total price
5926-82	L	Trousers	1	£ 25	£ 25
9115-30	M	T-shirt	2	£ 7	£ 14
				Subtotal	£ 39
				Postage	£ 4.50
				Total cost of goods	£ 43.50

> BrE: Freephone number; AmE: toll free number

30.1 Label the website extracts using words from the box. Look at A opposite to help you.

| bundles of items | delivery costs | payment options | product categories |

1

MasterCard
VISA

2

Standard (48 hours) = £1.50

Express (next day) = £2.50

Pick up at store = £1.00

3

Cameras ·······

Digital photo prints ·······

MP3 players ·······

4

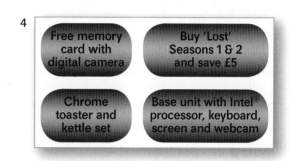

Free memory card with digital camera

Buy 'Lost' Seasons 1 & 2 and save £5

Chrome toaster and kettle set

Base unit with Intel® processor, keyboard, screen and webcam

30.2 Which of the services offered by an online store would be useful in these situations? Look at A opposite to help you.

1

2 I need it urgently – by tomorrow.

3

4 What would you like for your birthday, Jimmy?

30.3 The owner of a small business is thinking about putting her catalogue online, and is presenting the business case to her bank manager. Correct the mistakes in her PowerPoint slides. Look at B opposite to help you.

Pros

1 Customers can put an order 24 hours a day.

2 No need for already paid envelopes.

3 We can still have a hot telephone line.

4 The process of ordering will be much quicker.

Cons

5 The ordering form must be simplified for older users.

6 Older customers may prefer using mailing order to ordering online.

Over to you

Go to two online retailers and compare their sales process. Which one is easier to use? Why? How could you improve the other site's process?

31 Personal selling

A The sales force

The **sales representatives** or **salespeople** make up a company's **sales force**. They interact directly with customers or **prospects** – potential customers – to **make sales** and **build long-term relationships**.

The sales force can include **inside salespeople,** who conduct business from their offices, and **field salespeople** or **travelling salespeople,** who **call on customers** (visit them).

Sales forces are often organized with each salesperson having an **exclusive territory** – a geographical zone where they **make** their **sales calls** or **visits**. Salespeople normally receive **incentives** (see Unit 22), such as financial bonuses or gifts, if they **reach** their **target** or **sales quota** – the amount of revenue they have to bring in during a given period.

Note: **Sales rep** or **salesperson**? See Appendix I on page 108.

B Personal selling

Personal selling, or selling to a customer face-to-face, is different from **impersonal selling** such as advertising and sales promotion. Salespeople can **inform customers** and **demonstrate technical products**, at the same time **customizing the sales messages** to what that specific customer needs to hear.

C The sales process

The sales process helps the sales force **convert leads** into **signed deals** (change prospective customers to actual customers).

1 **Prospecting and qualifying**
   Salespeople **prospect** (or look for) new clients. New leads are generated by **making cold calls**, calling potential customers from a list (see Unit 29), or by **asking** current customers for **referrals**. The best leads are then identified, or **qualified**.

2 **Presenting**
   The sales presentation can focus on the product's USPs (see below), or be **customer-oriented** – showing how the product will **meet the customer's needs**. **Testimonials** from satisfied customers, **sales literature** and **samples** may support the presentation.

3 **Closing deals**
   When salespeople **spot**, or detect, **buying signals** from their customers, they will try to **close the deal** by asking the customer to **place an order**. They may **trade concessions** or **negotiate**.

4 **Following up**
   Follow-up calls are part of the **after-sales service** which enables salespeople to check **customer satisfaction with** the service or product – how happy they are with it. Satisfied customers will purchase again, **generating repeat business**.

D Marketing support

Marketing supports the sales force by providing **product knowledge** and **market knowledge** – information about what the sales force are selling and the environment they're selling it in. Marketers can design materials, or **marketing collateral**, to help the sales force present their **sales arguments**. The **sales kit** contains **sales aids** such as:

- **product samples** (so customers get a better idea of what the product is)
- **price lists** (so they can see how much it costs)
- **order forms** (so they can place an order)
- sales literature – brochures, leaflets and **product sheets** or **sales sheets**, containing information about the product **features** (what it does) and product **benefits** (why the product is good), and its **unique selling points** or USPs (what it has that its competitors don't).

31.1 Complete the crossword. All the answers make word combinations with *sales*. Look at A, B, C and D opposite to help you.

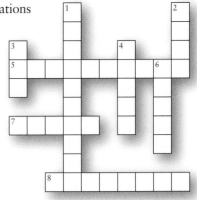

Across

5 We have a small sales force but we mostly invest in .... sales techniques such as advertising. (10)

7 Our incentive plan encourages the sales force to reach their sales .... (5)

8 The sales force listen to the customers and customize their sales .... to the customer needs. (8)

Down

1 Our sales .... includes product sheets and a new brochure with product information and testimonials. (10)

2 Each territory is quite large, so our salespeople only make one sales .... per day. (4)

3 The marketing team have designed a new sales .... for the product launch. (3)

4 There are 30 salespeople in our sales .... (5)

6 We have lost repeat business as we neglected our ....-sales service. (5)

31.2 Make word combinations using a word or phrase from each box. Then match some of the word combinations to the pictures below. Look at A and C opposite to help you.

ask	cold calls
close	buying signals
make	a deal
place	concessions
spot	for referrals
trade	an order

1

2

3

Over to you

Think of a product or a service that is usually sold by personal selling. Why is the sales method well suited to the product or service? What would you include in a sales kit for this product or service?

32 Above, below and through the line

A Above-the-line

Above-the-line (ATL) is a form of media advertising where a **commission** or fee is paid to an agency working for its clients. The commission represents a percentage of the **media investment** – that is, how much is spent on media during the **advertising campaign**.

ATL campaigns appear, or **run**, in **mainstream** or **mass media**. Examples include **commercials** on television, and **display ads** on billboards (see Unit 35 on outdoor advertising). ATL advertising is **interruptive**. For example, it is broadcast on TV in the advertising break in the middle of a programme and does not form part of the programme itself (see Unit 38 on branded content).

The **advertiser** (the client) **briefs**, or informs, the **advertising agency** (also known as the **ad agency**) on the **advertising objectives**. Typical objectives for an ATL campaign include making the customer aware of a product or service, or building the image of a brand. It is the role of the ad agency to develop an **advertising strategy** based on the client's **advertising brief**. The advertising strategy defines the **advertising messages** – what is to be communicated – and the choice of media. **Media planners**, working in the agency's media planning department or for a specialized **media agency**, define the **media strategy**, identifying appropriate channels to reach the target audience. The **media plan** includes the selection of specific **media vehicles** (for example, types of press magazines, TV channels, poster networks) and the **media schedule** (the times and dates when the advertising will appear). **Media buyers** negotiate with **advertising sales houses** or **advertising departments** to get the best price for the **media space** selected in the media plan (see Unit 33).

Note: Advertisements are more often referred to as **adverts** or **ads**.

B Below-the-line

Below-the-line (BTL) refers to any non-media advertising or promotion. **Marketing services agencies** are experts in **BTL tactics**, such as direct mail, exhibitions, point-of-sale, or street marketing (see Units 41–43). Marketing services agencies point to two trends that indicate that BTL spend will continue to grow:

1 **Ad avoidance** – consumers actively trying not to be exposed to advertising. **Ad avoiders** change channels during advertising breaks; this is sometimes known as **zapping**.
2 **Media fragmentation** – audiences are becoming smaller, or more **fragmented**, as the choice of media grows. Chris Anderson, editor-in-chief of *Wired* magazine, has invented the term **the Long Tail** to describe the growing number of sites on the internet with a small number of visitors. **Emerging media** (the internet, interactive TV, and virtual worlds such as Second Life) must now find ways to **tap into**, or exploit, the advertising opportunities in the Long Tail.

C Through-the-line

Some agencies now offer **through-the-line** (TTL), also known as **full services**. A **full service marketing agency** offers both ATL and BTL in **blended marketing**. TTL is also referred to as **holistic marketing** or **360 degree branding**. It uses **multi-channel marketing**, using both ATL and BTL communication channels to **build brands** (see Units 16–17). TTL can be very effective at **drawing attention to** your brand – getting people to notice it.

D Advertising techniques

Advertising uses different techniques to appeal to consumers. For a list, see Appendix VII on page 114.

32.1 Make sentences using one part from each column. Look at A, B and C opposite to help you. The first one has been done for you.

1

a Press	planners	are	media	agencies.
b Media	magazines	work in	media	vehicles.

a Press magazines are media vehicles.
b Media planners work in media agencies.

2

a Ad	marketing	uses	advertising	breaks.
b Blended	avoiders	zap during	TTL	techniques.

3

a Normally,	TV	is an	advertising	agencies.
b Interactive	advertisers	brief	emerging	media.

4

a Advertising	campaigns	don't run in	advertising	strategy.
b BTL	agencies	develop	mainstream	media.

32.2 In the description of Ford's promotional strategy, the underlined words and phrases are in the wrong place. Move them to the correct position. Look at A, B and C opposite to help you.

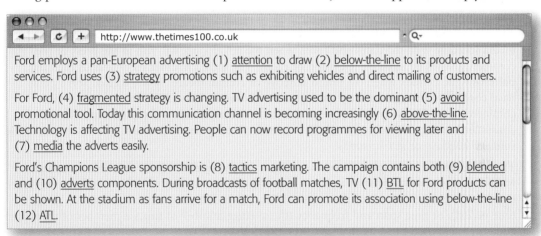

Ford employs a pan-European advertising (1) <u>attention</u> to draw (2) <u>below-the-line</u> to its products and services. Ford uses (3) <u>strategy</u> promotions such as exhibiting vehicles and direct mailing of customers.

For Ford, (4) <u>fragmented</u> strategy is changing. TV advertising used to be the dominant (5) <u>avoid</u> promotional tool. Today this communication channel is becoming increasingly (6) <u>above-the-line</u>. Technology is affecting TV advertising. People can now record programmes for viewing later and (7) <u>media</u> the adverts easily.

Ford's Champions League sponsorship is (8) <u>tactics</u> marketing. The campaign contains both (9) <u>blended</u> and (10) <u>adverts</u> components. During broadcasts of football matches, TV (11) <u>BTL</u> for Ford products can be shown. At the stadium as fans arrive for a match, Ford can promote its association using below-the-line (12) <u>ATL</u>.

32.3 Match the two parts of the sentences. Then decide if the sentences are true or false, according to 32.2 above. Look at the page opposite and Appendix VII on page 114 to help you.

1 Ford is using the internet to tap
2 Ford is only using interruptive
3 Ford is using pester
4 Ford is using multi-channel
5 Ford has display

a marketing.
b adverts at football stadiums.
c advertising on the TV.
d power, by appealing to children.
e into the Long Tail.

Over to you

Think about some advertisements or promotions you have seen recently. Was ATL, BTL or TTL used?

33 Media strategy

A Media strategy

The **media strategy** is part of the marketing plan. It recommends how to deliver brand messages to the consumer in a way that best serves the brand's **communication objectives**, such as building loyalty, encouraging purchase or aiding brand recognition. The media strategy identifies the right **target audience** (the people the brand wants to talk to) and the **media mix** (the combination of media types – press, outdoor or internet) which will be used to deliver the messages. The target audience is described in terms of **lifestyle** (the way people live) and **demographics** (their gender, age, ethnicity, education and income). The **media split** gives the breakdown of the **media budget** – the amount of money allocated to the campaign – between different media types – for example, 70% of investment on television and 30% in the press.

In a **media-saturated world**, where media is everywhere, it is difficult to **stand out** from rival advertising, or be noticed, so brands need to identify the best **touchpoints** – places to reach their **core target**, or main audience. Media strategists use **media research**, based on interviews, surveys and measurement tools, to get information about the impact of the different media types, and to get **insights into**, or understanding of, the **media consumption habits** of their target audience. Children's food brands often advertise on television because women with children are **heavy TV viewers** – that is, they watch a lot of television. A cinema campaign may be more efficient to reach **light TV viewers** as the audience is **captive** and **attentive** – they're sitting in the cinema, waiting for the film to start.

B Media planning

The **media plan** recommends **communication channels** with the names of specific publications, TV channels or other **media vehicles** to be used for the campaign. The plan includes a **media schedule** with the dates and times when the advertising will **run in the press** or the commercials will be **aired on television** or **radio**. The **media planner** recommends **flighting patterns** – the periods when the brand is active or communicates in the media. Some plans have **continuity strategies** or **drip strategies**. For example, a detergent manufacturer airs commercials on TV every day for several months to keep the brand **top of mind** – fresh in consumers' memories. Other brands have **bursts** of heavy **media pressure** – for example, in the summer holidays or at Christmas.

The media plan must respect the media budget and the **media objectives** for the campaign. Media objectives are defined in terms of **impressions** (the number of times an ad is seen), **reach** or **coverage** (the percentage of the target audience exposed to an advertisement in a given time period), or **time span** and **frequency** (the average number of times a member of the target audience is exposed to an ad in a given time period).

C Media buying

When the plan is **approved by** the client, the **media buyer** makes the **media bookings** (reserves **space** in magazines or **airtime** on television) and produces a media schedule. TV media buyers now have software to **optimize their plans** – that is, to make the best choice of channels and commercial breaks.

Media planners and buyers are **accountable to** their clients. Costs and results of campaigns are measured (see Unit 24). **Cost per thousand** (CPM) is a standard measure of media efficiency; it is the amount an advertiser pays for one thousand impressions. Big clients can organize **media audits** to **benchmark**, or compare, the cost and results of their campaigns with those of their competitors.

Note: The singular noun is **medium** and the **plural** is media.

Medium	Audience
TV (see Unit 34)	viewers
radio (see Unit 34)	listeners
outdoor (see Unit 35)	audience
press (see Unit 36)	readers
cinema	cinema-goers
internet (see Unit 39)	users or surfers

33.1 Complete the notes on a media strategy using words from the box. One word can be used twice. Look at A and B opposite to help you.

core	impressions	media	reach
demographics	lifestyle	objectives	research
habits	light	plan	target

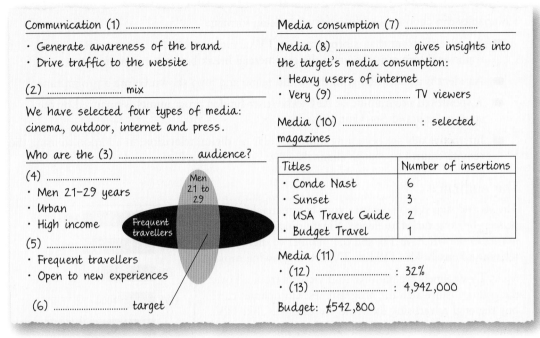

Communication (1) ....

· Generate awareness of the brand
· Drive traffic to the website

(2) .... mix

We have selected four types of media: cinema, outdoor, internet and press.

Who are the (3) .... audience?

(4) ....
· Men 21–29 years
· Urban
· High income

(5) ....
· Frequent travellers
· Open to new experiences

(6) .... target

Media consumption (7) ....

Media (8) .... gives insights into the target's media consumption:
· Heavy users of internet
· Very (9) .... TV viewers

Media (10) .... : selected magazines

Titles	Number of insertions
· Conde Nast	6
· Sunset	3
· USA Travel Guide	2
· Budget Travel	1

Media (11) ....
· (12) .... : 32%
· (13) .... : 4,942,000

Budget: $542,800

33.2 Choose the correct words from the brackets to complete the sentences. Look at A, B and C opposite to help you.

1 We studied the competitors' flighting (patterns / audience / touchpoints) before selecting a drip (pattern / burst / strategy) to give constant media pressure throughout the year.
2 (Reach / Cost / Frequency) per thousand is the amount paid to reach 1,000 people. It can be used to compare the cost effectiveness of different media (planners / pressure / vehicles).
3 A huge media (budget / buyer / mix) is necessary to keep our brand top of (booking / viewers / mind). It is difficult to stand out with so many competitors airing (commercials / benchmarks / touchpoints) on television.
4 We invested in new software to help media buyers (approve / optimize / air) our media plan.
5 The advertiser organized a media (schedule / strategy / audit) to assess the effectiveness of our media buying and planning. Unfortunately, we were less efficient than our competitors.

33.3 Match the two parts of the sentences. Look at C opposite to help you.

1 The media plan must be approved
2 We use media research to get insights
3 The media buyer is accountable
4 This campaign will run
5 Airtime

a to the client.
b on television can be very expensive.
c by the client before we make any bookings.
d into the viewing habits of our target audience.
e in the national press.

Over to you

You are organizing an award event to reward innovative and effective media planning. Think about advertising and communication campaigns you have seen recently and make a shortlist of recipients for the award.

34 TV and radio

A Advertising on TV or radio

If a company wishes to **advertise on TV** or **radio**, the first step is usually to contact an **advertising agency**, who will **produce the ad**. They will **come up with a communication strategy**; this includes advertising **copy** for an advert (the text), and perhaps a **catchy jingle** (memorable music for your ad) or a memorable **slogan** (for example, Gillette's 'The best a man can get').

Companies can choose from different advertising formats:

- An advertisement that is **broadcast on TV** or **radio** is called a **commercial** or an **ad**. This traditional format is shown in the **commercial break** between programmes.
- An **ident** is a short film with the brand name and logo shown before a programme.
- A **sponsored programme** or **AFP** (**advertiser-funded programme**) is financed by the sponsor or brand (see Unit 38).
- **Interactive ads** are becoming more popular on **digital television**; in addition to using the **remote control** to change channels, viewers can press a button and respond to an ad.

B The audience

The second step is to make sure your commercial is heard or seen by your target audience. Ninety-nine percent of homes in the UK have TV, and the number of digital **television households** (**TVH** or **TVHH**) is growing rapidly.

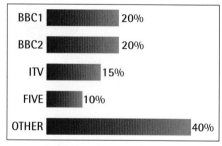

BBC1	20%
BBC2	20%
ITV	15%
FIVE	10%
OTHER	40%

British TV channels: audience share

Most **TV channels** are national and **viewers** from all over the country can watch the programmes. Companies can buy **regional advertising** for some TV channels (like ITV in the UK) or **national advertising** if they want to **reach** the whole country. **Local radio stations** attract **listeners** from only one area.

The **audience profile** gives information about the **listeners** or **viewers**, including age, sex and possibly income. The **viewing** or **listening figures** show how large the audience is for a certain programme or for a whole channel or station. **The GRP** (**gross rating points**) show the percentage of the target audience **reached** by a television commercial. **Television ratings** (**TVR**) show the relative popularity of different TV programmes. Ratings differ from **audience share**, which refers to the percentage of total audience watching TV at any one moment who are viewing a given channel. For example, an audience share of 65% for a football match shows that 65% of people watching TV at that time were watching the football match.

The big channels for each country are called **mainstream media**. They feature general programmes and **cater for** everyone, providing what people want or need to see. Customers can pay to subscribe to **cable TV** and **satellite TV**. **Terrestrial TV**, which is broadcast via radio waves, is usually free, or **free-to-air**. Channel 4 in the UK is an example of a terrestrial channel. Some national TV channels, like the BBC, are funded by a **TV licence fee**, which all households with a TV set must pay.

C Dayparts

Dayparts are sections of the day during which **programmes** are **broadcast** or **aired** to appeal to the particular demographic group that will be watching or listening. Most people have regular **listening** or **viewing habits** and will usually watch, or **tune in to**, the same programmes every day or week.

For names of dayparts and descriptions of audiences and programmes, see Appendix VIII on page 115.

34.1 Match the words and phrases (1–5) to the definitions (a–e). Look at A, B and C opposite to help you.

1 advertiser-funded programmes
2 audience
3 commercial break
4 daypart
5 free-to-air

a TV channels offered free to users, without subscription
b the population or target group viewing a television programme or an advertisement
c shows which are fully or partly paid for by an advertiser
d a broadcast time period, e.g. daytime: 0900–1630
e the time during which ads are shown between programmes

34.2 Complete the texts about TV and radio advertising using words from the box. Look at A and B opposite to help you.

channels	listeners	programmes	reaching	station

TV plays a huge role in our lives and even in these days of 200-plus (1) .... , ITV1 continues to be the most watched. In 2005, a massive 885 of the 1,000 highest-rating (2) .... were shown on ITV1.

Classic FM is the largest commercial radio (3) .... in the UK,
(4) .... almost 6 million people every week. Most of the station's
(5) .... are not connoisseurs of classical music and come to us because
of the way Classic FM makes them feel, regardless of age, sex or income.

34.3 Make word combinations using a word from each box. Some words can be used more than once. Look at A, B and C opposite and Appendix VIII on page 115 to help you.

commercial	reality
game	remote
listening	soap
prime	TV
radio	weather

break	opera
channel	show
control	station
forecast	time
habits	TV

Over to you

Keep an advertising diary for two days and note all the types of advertising you see on television and hear on the radio. Write down the type of station or channel, the daypart, the type of programme and the type of product or service being advertised. Do you see any patterns?

Time	Channel	Daypart	Programme	Product / Service

35 Outdoor advertising

A Out-of-home advertising formats

Outdoor advertising, or **out-of-home (OOH) advertising** can really grab your attention or **get in your face**. Advertisers have a wide choice of poster sites, sizes and formats from 4 **sheets** to 96 sheets (see table).

Roadside panels: Billboards are large outdoor panels for displaying ads. **Giant banners** or **wallscapes** are **hung** on the front of buildings. Outdoor contractors also offer **lightboxes** (illuminated panels), **tri-face billboards** (with rotating sections allowing three different advertisements to be displayed in sequence) and **scrollers** (signs displaying a number of posters, one after the other).

Panel size	Size (inches)
4 sheet:	60 × 40
6 sheet:	72 × 48
12 sheet:	120 × 60
16 sheet:	120 × 80
48 sheet:	120 × 240
96 sheet	480 × 120

Street furniture: In 1962 Jean-Claude Decaux introduced the concept of advertising on **bus shelters. Pedestrian panels** are **backlit** – lit from behind – and normally located on streets in town and city centres.

Transit advertising: Taxis, buses, trams and trains can be **wrapped** in **vinyl** showing a company's adverts. Ads can also be positioned **inside** or on the **side** or **rear** of a vehicle.

Ambient media: Adverts can be displayed on non-traditional media such as the back of a receipt from a shop or a travel ticket. The use of **floor graphics** is common in supermarkets and shopping centres.

Digital outdoor advertising: LED screens are used in similar sites to traditional billboards. **Digital video billboards** show short advertising spots (15, 30 or 60 seconds). Consumers can **interact** directly with some **interactive** advertising sites, such as bus shelters and poster panels, using their mobile phones.

A wallscape and a wrapped vehicle

For illustrations of OOH advertising, see Appendix IX on page 116.

Note: Paste is the adhesive used to attach posters to walls; the word can be used as a noun and as a verb. Billboards are sometimes called **hoardings** in India and the UK.

B Effectiveness of OOH

Advertisers can buy a **network of sites** to target their consumers or to reach people in their geographical area, or **catchment zone**.

Eye-catching – attractive and noticeable – ads such as **sonic posters** (which include sounds), **'smelly' posters** (including smells or odours) and **lenticular posters** (showing different images as you walk past them) can be very memorable.

Outdoor campaigns can be measured by **opportunities to see (OTS)** or **coverage** (see Unit 33). The term **approach** specifies the distance between the point where the advertisement first become visible, to the point where is no longer readable because it has passed out of sight.

35.1 Complete the crossword. Look at A and B opposite to help you.

Across

2 Another name for a hoarding. (9)
5 This type of furniture is found outside. (6)
7 This type of advertising makes a noise. (5)
8 A giant .... is hung on a building. (6)
10 Advertising on buses, taxis, etc. (7)
12 Advertising you can walk on: a .... graphic. (5)
13 The latest technology for out-of-home advertising. (7)
14 The image changes as you walk past this type of poster. (10)

Down

1 Out-of-home advertising gets in your .... (4)
3 To put up posters. (5)
4 An illuminated panel. (8)
6 By the sides of streets and roads. (8)
9 You can wrap buses and taxis in this material. (5)
11 Another word for 'out-of-home'. (7)

35.2 Complete the news report using words from the box. Look at A and B opposite to help you.

catching	coverage	graphics	hung	shelters	wrapped

Commuters in Bristol were surprised by an invasion of out-of-home advertising last Tuesday. The opening of a new concert hall was announced by huge banners (1) .... on prominent sites around the city. Buses were (2) .... in the concert hall's logo and colours. Bus (3) .... were treated to new eye- (4) .... interactive ads that lit up and made noises as pedestrians walked past. A spokesperson for the new concert hall said that the public reaction had been good. 'We got greater (5) .... than we had imagined.' he added. One commuter said that she had been pleasantly surprised to find herself walking on floor (6) .... instead of the ordinary floor.

A digital billboard

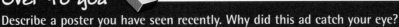

Over to you

Describe a poster you have seen recently. Why did this ad catch your eye?

36 The press

A Newspapers

Most newspapers are **dailies**, printed every day. Some are **weeklies**, printed once a week. The **national daily press** includes titles like *The Sun* and *The Times* in the UK and is available all over the country. The **regional press** is only available in certain parts of the country – for example, the *South Wales Echo*. The **local press** is similar to the regional press but for a smaller geographical area – for example, the *Basingstoke Gazette* is only for sale in the town of Basingstoke.

Tabloids are newspapers with a smaller format than **broadsheets**. Originally broadsheets carried more economic and political reports and were more serious. Most UK newspapers today are tabloid or **Berliner**, slightly bigger than a tabloid. However, the term **tabloid press** is still used to refer to less serious newspapers which contain sensational stories, short **articles** or reports, and a lot of photographs. Some newspapers are not sold but given away free. These **freesheets** are funded entirely by the **advertising** they **carry**.

B Magazines

Magazines can be **weekly**, published every week; **fortnightly**, published every two weeks; or **monthly**, published every month.

For descriptions and illustrations of different categories of magazines, see Appendix X on page 117.

C Choosing titles

The **advertising sales** department of a newspaper or magazine sells **advertising space** or **advertising positions** in their publications. As part of the sales effort, ad salespeople work with the marketing team to prepare **media packs**, which contain information about:

- The **advertising rates,** or cost of advertising in the newspaper or magazine. The **rate card** shows the price of advertising and also gives **technical data** about the size, or **format**, of the ad. The **copy deadline** tells advertisers when they have to deliver the **copy** (the images and text for the ad) or the complete advert itself.

- **Circulation figures** or **distribution figures**, showing the number of **copies** (single newspapers or magazines) sold per **issue** (the version of the newspaper or magazine published on a particular date). The **readership figures**, which show how many people read the publication, may be higher than the circulation figures because one **copy** may be read by more than one person.

- The **advertising policy** of the publication, which gives general information on what can be advertised, which formats are available, and how to pay.

- Details and dates about **special features** – articles about a particular subject, such as the Technology Quarterly from *The Economist*, or reviews of fashion shows in women's magazines. If you are a clothing brand it is a good idea to **book space** to coincide with reviews of fashion shows.

D Choosing a position

The price of an ad varies depending on the position in the newspaper or magazine. See Appendix XI on page 118 for the rate card from a local British newspaper.

36.1 Match the categories of newspapers and magazines (1–6) to the descriptions (a–f). Look at A and B opposite and Appendix X on page 117 to help you.

1 daily local freesheet
2 fortnightly special interest
3 monthly children's magazine
4 monthly glossy men's magazine
5 regional daily press
6 weekly national press

a Since October 10, 1870, the *Eastern Daily Press* has been a source of authoritative comment for its readers in Norfolk, North Suffolk and East Cambridgeshire, helping form opinion and encourage debate.
b A leading quality magazine, whether it's fashion, sport, health, humour, politics or music, every month *GQ* covers it all with intelligence and imagination.
c *The Sunday Review* from *The Independent* is part of the 'world's best designed newspaper'. It is renowned for its strong reporting, national news features and cultured outlook.
d *RAIL* is published twice a month in the UK. It is Britain's number one modern rail magazine for news, features, analysis and opinion. Perfect for the railway enthusiast.
e *CY* – A brilliant new intelligent and entertaining magazine for 7 to 12-year-old children. Full of features, activities, puzzles, facts, cartoons and challenges to stimulate and stretch their minds. 12 issues a year.
f *Metro* is designed to be read in about 20 minutes and contains bite-sized national and international news and local information – entertainment previews, listings, weather and travel. We're completely free and you can pick us up Monday to Friday in 15 cities across the country.

36.2 Choose the correct word combinations from the brackets to complete the sentences. There are two possible answers for each question. Look at C opposite to help you.

1 Our (copy deadline is / circulation figures are / readership is) growing year on year.
2 You can book (advertising positions / advertising space / advertising policy) using our secure online booking system.
3 Please click here to download a PDF version of our (media pack / book space / rate card).
4 Before submitting an ad, please make sure you have read and understood the (technical data / advertising space / advertising rates).

36.3 Make word combinations using a word or phrase from each box. One word can be used twice. Look at Appendix XI on page 118 to help you.

centre
facing
front page
full
half

matter
page
solus
spread

Over to you

Collect some newspapers and magazines, and select an ad. Which format has the advertiser used? Why do you think they have selected this publication and this format?

37 Printed documents

A Design

Printed documents (or printed material) are usually prepared by a graphic studio. Graphic designers design the page, or layout, and prepare a dummy or a mock-up which shows how the finished job will look. They work to graphic guidelines to ensure that all the marketing collateral (which includes sales aids such as brochures and magazine ad inserts) has the same look.

The copy (the text) is written directly by the marketing team, or by specialized copywriters working for a communications agency. This process is known as copywriting. The copy is proofread to find and correct mistakes.

B Preparing to print

The graphic chain refers to the process of printing documents, or the print job, from the initial contact with the printers to the final run when the finished material is printed. The process starts with establishing an estimate, the price for the print job. The print run, or number of documents to be printed, must also be decided. A long run prints a large number of documents. Some printers accept short runs of only ten documents.

It is important to fix or set deadlines for job completion. It is also essential to respect deadlines so that each stage of the job is completed on time.

C The print job

There are four stages to a print job:

1 **Prepress**, the first stage, covers all the work before printing happens. This includes **typesetting**, also known as **composition**, which is arranging the text and **artwork** (photos and illustrations) on the page. **Print specifications** – prepress guidelines including colour references and dimensions – must be followed. **Registration marks**, showing how to line up the colours on a page, and **crop marks**, showing where to cut, or **crop**, the paper, should also be included.
2 **Final proofing**, the second stage, involves checking the print job. At the end of this process, the client will **sign off the job** and agree that no further **amendments**, or corrections, need to be **made**. Marketers are often responsible for this 'proof OK'. A **press check** is run: a few copies are printed and checked for **colour correction**, to make sure the colours are right.
3 The third stage, known as **printing** or 'the press', involves transferring **ink** to a material such as paper, plastic or metal. There are several different printing techniques and colour options.

   - **Silk screen:** used to produce multicoloured designs for flat surfaces, like signs or CDs.
   - **Lithographic:** used for large quantities of printed material such as brochures.
   - **Hot stamping:** a more expensive technique used to print in gold, silver or other foils and metallic papers.
   - **Embossing:** creating a raised mark on the material.
   - **Digital printing:** specifically dedicated to short runs; data and images are printed directly from a computer file.
   - **Full colour** can be achieved by the **four colour process**, or CMYK (cyan, magenta, yellow, and key / black). The **six colour process**, or **Hexachrome**, developed by Pantone, uses CMYKOG – orange and green are added to make more vibrant colours.
   - **Spot colours**, exclusively made inks, cannot be reproduced by the four colour process.
   - **Black and white** (b/w) printing; **mono**, or **one colour**, printing sometimes uses black ink.

4 **Finishing**, the final stage, may include **perfect binding** (joining several pages together into a book, brochure or catalogue), **folding** (bending the paper onto itself) or **perforating** (making small holes in the material – for example, for money-off vouchers or response cards).

37.1 Make word combinations using a word from each box. Then use the combinations to complete the description of a print job. Look at A, B and C opposite to help you.

graphic	OK
job	a deadline
long	designer
press	run
printed	check
proof	completion
set	material

Objective

Hotel group Queen's Moat House Hotels UK wanted to attract more families with children in the three to ten years age group. Moat Houses (1) .... for (2) .... for early spring.

Solution

With no previous history in this sector a brand had to be created from scratch. Our (3) .... created three mediaeval characters, Sir Quintin Malpas Hump, his servant Morris, and a dragon called Henry. The initials of each of the first names being QMH, representing those of Queen's Moat Houses. The trio have subsequently featured in other (4) .... : comics, paper hats, and posters to name but a few items – all designed and produced by HOA. After (5) .... from Queen's Moat House Hotels we launched a (6) .... to validate the colours.

Result

All of the items that HOA produced were very much in demand, to the point that many of them became collector's items. We are currently working on a summer menu for the hotels. This print job will have a (7) .... as the previous items have been so popular.

37.2 Replace the underlined words and expressions with alternative words and expressions from A and C opposite.

1 <u>Printed material that helps sell a product</u> leaves a lasting impression on your clients.
2 You can trust our <u>writing</u> skills to create fantastic-sounding arguments.
3 We will guide and assist you in all stages of the <u>printing work</u>.
4 We print in <u>blue, pink, yellow and black</u>.
5 After the <u>period of checking and amending the print job</u>, the client <u>tells the printer to start printing</u>.

Embossing

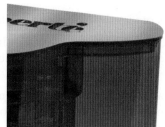
Hot stamping

Perforating

Over to you

Find a printed document that you think is effective. What is the purpose of the document and who is the target? Describe:

■ the layout   ■ the artwork   ■ the copy   ■ the finish.

38 Branded content

A History of branded content

Branded content is **entertainment** created, funded or produced by a brand. For example, Nestlé's Purina pet food produces a TV show called *Talk to the Animals*, which has stories about animals and advice on feeding cats and dogs. **Brand messages** or **values** are integrated into the content of an **entertainment property**, which could be a TV show, a video game, a book or a live event.

The entertainment property is often **co-created** or **co-produced** by the brand. The brand sometimes **barters**, or exchanges, the entertainment property for **airtime** – commercial space on television or radio.

Branded content has grown due to **media fragmentation** (see Unit 32). With more and more TV channels, websites and magazines, it has become more difficult for advertisers to reach their target audiences with conventional **interruptive advertising** such as commercials in advertising breaks. However, by providing content, the brand **engages** and **connects with** consumers, offering an emotional encounter with the brand, or a **brand experience**, rather than just exposure to an advertising message.

B Types of branded content

Advertiser-funded programmes: the name for branded content on TV and radio, this is now a common feature of the audio-visual landscape. The travel agent, Thomas Cook, has even become a **media owner**, with initiatives such as Thomas Cook TV, which broadcasts programmes about holiday destinations.

Off-air events: brands organize shows or events, such as the Nokia Urban Music Festival.

Digital media networks: this has screens with information, news or entertainment in public places such as train stations. Tesco has **captive audience networks** in its stores.

Online: the interactivity of online platforms (see Unit 39) allows brands to **create a dialogue with** consumers and even to display, or **post**, written or video **user-generated content** (content developed by visitors to the site). Land Rover's internet TV channel, for example, encourages viewers to **share their content** by uploading their own films.

Mobile or **wireless content:** brands provide content such as mobile games, logos and ringtones.

Contract publishing: many brands have gone beyond producing **advertorials** – advertising in a newspaper or magazine presented to resemble an editorial article. Some brands are now producing **consumer magazines** which increase the time the consumer spends with the brand.

Films: BMW **commissioned** a series of films by Hollywood producers starring their cars.

Advergaming: embedding, or integrating, **the brand values** in **advergames** – video games produced by advertisers – enables advertisers to reach young adults, who often avoid conventional advertising.

Product placement or **integration:** a product or a **product reference** (when someone mentions the product) appears in an entertainment property. Product placement has been common since the 1960s, when Sean Connery was seen driving an Aston Martin in a James Bond film.

C Efficiency

Marketers need to ensure that branded content **serves the marketing communication objectives** (see Unit 33) as well as the editorial needs of the broadcaster. Branded content can generate huge **media exposure** (reach a lot of people), and achieve **media standout** – get the brand noticed. Some advertisers assess media efficiency by calculating the cost of buying **equivalent airtime** – that is, the same amount of airtime using conventional advertising.

38.1 Choose the correct words from the brackets to complete the articles about branded content. Look at A and B opposite to help you.

1 BMW have (commissioned / sharing / embedding) contemporary authors to write downloadable audio books filled with intrigue and suspense. The stories are (boosted / co-produced / entertained) with the publisher Random House. This is another example of BMW using (branded entertainment / contract publishing / advergaming) to engage with consumers.

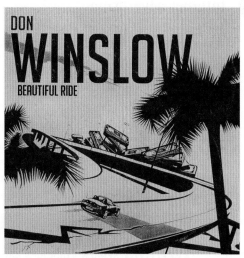

DON
WINSLOW
BEAUTIFUL RIDE

BMW audio book

2 The Coca-Cola Company has teamed up with Smartphones Technologies to deliver Coca-Cola polar bears and other Coke (branded content / advertorials / captive audience networks) to cell phones. Smartphones will also create Coca-Cola (off-air events / mobile content / user-generated content) such as video ringtones and mobile games. Coke has universal brand recognition and is offering the consumers a brand (experience / value / reference) that will boost the perception of the brand.

3 (Contract publishing / Product placement / Wireless content) has become commonplace in movies and TV shows. Now it's coming to comic books – DC Comics is launching a new series which showcases General Motors' car, the Pontiac Solstice. The hero, known as 'The Rush', will be seen driving the car. DC Comics is promoting their title as a place to (engage with / volunteer / share) young men in their 20s.

38.2 Complete the quotes using words from the box. Look at A and C opposite to help you.

airtime	connects	generated	standout
barter	exposure	share	communication

1 Branded entertainment can help a brand achieve media .... in a world with increasing media choice.

2 We establish the price of a 30-second commercial and then calculate the value of the .... we .... in exchange for the programme.

3 If your marketing .... objectives are to change attitudes and increase awareness, the media .... you get from product placement could be very useful.

4 User-............................ content is very effective. It's not expensive for us to produce, the users love to .... their films by uploading them, and it really .... with our target.

Over to you

Imagine that you are participating in a conference about branded content. Write a short speech entitled: 'Is branded content the future?'

39 The internet

A Internet advertising

Some of the most common internet advertising formats are **banners, buttons** and **skyscrapers** (see below). Other formats include:

- **Pop-ups** – new windows that open on your screen as you surf the web.
- **Microsites** – small websites (which may be part of a large website) dedicated to promoting a specific product or event. A microsite has its own address or URL.
- **Rich media formats** – animated, highly interactive advertisements.

The effectiveness of an **online ad unit** or **online advertising vehicle** is measured in **impressions** – the number of times that the ad is shown to an **online audience**. A good campaign will use **contextual technology** to deliver ads to web pages that are relevant to the target audience.

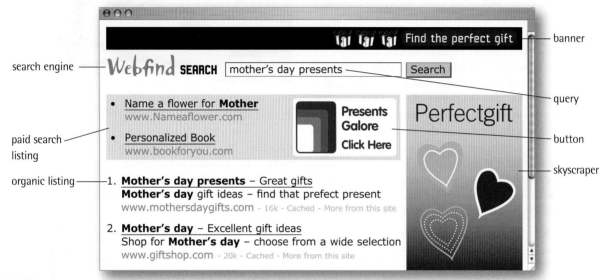

B Search engines

A **search engine**, such as Google or Yahoo! Search, allows users to look for specific information on the web. Search engines **list** relevant websites, or return **search listings**, in response to a user **query** – a **keyword** or **search term** typed into the **search box**.

Search engines are interesting to marketers as they provide **targeted traffic** – when a consumer searches the web, they may be ready to purchase a product or service (see Unit 20).

C Search engine marketing

Search engine marketing (**SEM**) includes:

- **paid search** – in addition to the **organic listings** or **unpaid search listings**, brands can pay search engines to display advertising in the form of sponsored links or **paid search listings**.
- **search engine optimization** (**SEO**) – increasing the number of visitors, or **traffic,** to a website by improving the **ranking** of the website. This means getting a search engine **to rank** the website **high** on the **search engine results page** (**SERP**).

SEO techniques are classified as **white hat** if they are recommended by search engines as part of good web page design, and **black hat** if they are disapproved of by search engines. **Keyword stuffing** is an example of a black hat technique: a web page is loaded up with keywords to mislead the search engine about the content or interest of the website.

39.1 Make word combinations with *search* using words from the box. Some words cannot be used, and some can be used more than once. Look at A, B and C opposite to help you.

banner	keywords	page	traffic
box	listings	paid	terms
engine	marketing	results	unpaid
hat	optimization	skyscraper	user

....
....

(search)

....
....
....
....
....
....
....

39.2 What do these abbreviations stand for? Look at B and C opposite to help you.

SEO ....

SEM ....

SERP ....

39.3 In the description of SEO, the underlined words and phrases are in the wrong place. Move them to the correct position. Look at B and C opposite to help you.

SEO is short for search (1) <u>rank</u> optimization. The objective is to increase the number of visitors to a website by improving the site's (2) <u>SERP</u> in the (3) <u>engine</u> returned by search engines.

We are a leading (4) <u>listings</u> company with many years of experience in the field. We understand how search engines (5) <u>ranking</u> web pages. Our experts follow SEO news and help keep our client's websites at the top of the (6) <u>SEO</u>.

How do we do it? This sounds like a simple question but …

39.4 Choose the correct words from the brackets to complete the sentences. Look at B and C opposite to help you.

1 Some marketers pay search engines to (rank / ranking) their website higher.
2 SEO uses keywords to get a better (rank / ranking).
3 Black hat SEO uses trick techniques to get a higher (rank / ranking).
4 Users usually look at the websites that (rank / ranking) at the top of the results page.

Over to you

Which ad formats do you see most often on the internet? Why do you think these formats are so popular?

40 Buzz marketing

A Word of mouth

Marketing has relied on **word of mouth** (**WOM**) for a long time – happy consumers have always told their friends about the products they like. Direct marketing (see Unit 29) often includes **testimonials** from ordinary people or the **general public** who say why they like using the product. **Favourable word of mouth publicity** – positive WOM – is highly beneficial for the brand because the person who **spreads the word** is usually **highly trusted** – a family member, for example. However, the product or service must not disappoint the **target audience** – it must **live up to the hype** created by WOM.

B Buzz marketing and stealth marketing

Buzz marketing uses existing **networks**, often **social networks** (for example, groups of friends), to increase brand awareness. **Social networking** relies on the idea that people will **pass along** and share cool and entertaining content. Unlike word of mouth, **buzz** is **generated** by the brand itself, looking to build awareness of a product or service. A **buzz marketing campaign** hopes that the message will spread quickly, thanks to **buzz agents**, people who pass along messages.

CommentUK is a company which specializes in **live buzz**. This is done by **performers** (actors) acting out live advertisements. To promote the Nintendo Wii, teams of performers visited cinemas, **interacted with** other cinemagoers, and played a game live on the big screen.

Brands also use **stealth marketing**, where consumers are not aware that they are being marketed to. For example, Sony promoted a camera-phone using actors who pretended to be tourists. The actors asked people to take pictures of them, and took the opportunity to **praise the brand**, saying positive things about it.

Live buzz

C Electronic buzz

An **electronic buzz marketing campaign**, also known as **viral marketing**, uses **viral commercials** – ads which are sent around the internet by users themselves. The commercials could be funny **video clips** (short video files), **interactive Flash games**, images, or any content people would be inclined to **share** with others. These campaigns can be started by email, in **chat rooms** or on **discussion boards** where groups of people with shared interests meet online, and on **peer to peer sites** such as YouTube.

At the end of a viral commercial there is usually a **clickable link** to 'tell a friend' or 'email this page'. The success of an electronic campaign can be measured by the number of **emails opened**, the **click-through rate** – how many people clicked on the link after opening the mail – and the number of **pass-along events** (emails sent to contacts).

D Generating a buzz

This extract is from the website of Outstanda, an internet marketing agency:

> Buzz marketing is a strategy that will **get you talked about**, and in the news. Outstanda specializes in helping clients generate more buzz on the web. We will **create** a little **buzz** each day. We will add to the buzz with **press releases** and by cultivating relationships with **bloggers**. We help you identify what makes you **buzzworthy** – worth talking about.
>
> Many **buzz efforts** take at least four weeks of planning and much more time for the story to **catch on**, or become popular.

Note: For more information on **press releases**, see Unit 47. For more on **bloggers**, see Unit 50.

40.1 Make word combinations using a word from each box. Then use the correct forms of some of the combinations to complete the sentences below. Look at A, B and C opposite to help you.

chat	social
general	spread the
live up to	stealth
pass	target
peer to	word of

along	word
audience	public
mouth	peer
the hype	networks
marketing	room

1 City dwellers are increasingly buying food products direct from farmers. Sixty-six percent of customers said they had heard about the farm they use by ....

2 Three mothers created a line of clothing for kids called Mum's The Word in 1995. They dressed their own kids in Mum's The Word clothes; the kids became brand ambassadors and .... about the new brand.

3 One of the most difficult aspects of viral marketing is making sure the product or service .... and doesn't disappoint the consumers when they actually try it.

4 Advertisers are starting to use .... The brand sends a message to a limited number of influencers, who spread the message to their network.

40.2 Match the two parts of the sentences. Look at A, B, C and D opposite to help you.

1 Procter & Gamble has released viral

2 In addition to launching the Noscruf.org website, the campaign includes paid search ads, and two viral videos on the peer

3 The Sony Bravia advert with paint exploding over a block of flats spread

4 The general

5 The film has been uploaded onto peer to peer sites and widely discussed in chat

6 The JetBlue airline recruited a network of buzz

7 Influential students pass

8 A portal allows ambassadors to share ideas and communicate with other students in their social

a agents called CrewBlue Campus Ambassadors.

b rooms.

c along the airline's brand message on university campuses.

d public was allowed to attend the shooting of the new campaign and the film was released on the Bravia website.

e commercials that aim to persuade men to shave.

f on the internet.

g to peer site YouTube.com.

h networks.

The Sony Bravia advert

Over to you

The Federal Trade Commission (FTC) is opposed to stealth marketing. Find three arguments for and three arguments against stealth marketing.

Sales promotions and displays

A Sales promotions

Marketers and consumers are people talking about **sales promotions**:

> We run a **prize draw**, or competition, every year in the summer. It's **free to enter**, so we have to label the packs with **no purchase necessary** to show that consumers don't have to buy the product to enter. This year we're thinking of changing the rules. We'd like to include **an element of skill** by asking the **entrants** to answer a simple question in order to take part. This way we can require a **proof of purchase**, like a receipt, from the entrants.

> I bought these biscuits because I had a **money-off coupon**. Thirty pence off, now that's not bad. My son got it from the internet. It's one of these new **e-coupons**. You know – an **online coupon**.

> I always buy my shampoo when there is a **special offer**, like **three for two**. It's even better if it's **buy one get one free**, or BOGOF.

> As the marketing manager for a breakfast cereal, I like to use **gifts with purchase** to target children. We often put a small plastic toy inside the packet. (See Unit 27)

> My local supermarket always goes crazy in the summer with **seasonal promotions** for sun cream and leg wax. Sometimes you can't find the milk because of all the **in-store promotions**.

BrE: prize draw; AmE: sweepstake

B Point of purchase (POP) or point of sale (POS) displays

Display units come in a variety of shapes and sizes. It is possible to **display** the products themselves, product information and advertising.

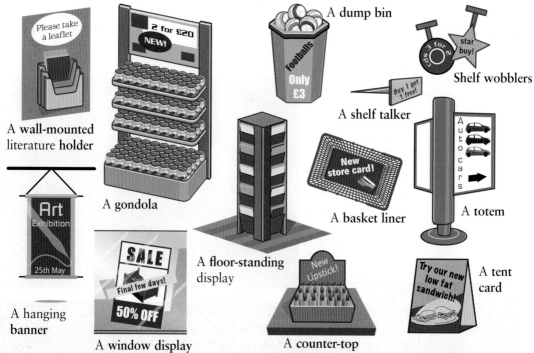

Please take a leaflet

2 for £20 NEW!

A dump bin

£3 for 2 · star buy!

Shelf wobblers

Footballs Only £3

Buy 1 get 1 free!

A shelf talker

A wall-mounted literature **holder**

Art Exhibition 25th May

A gondola

New store card!

A basket liner

Autocars

A totem

A floor-standing display

A hanging banner

SALE Final few days! 50% OFF

A window display

New Lipstick!

A counter-top display

Try our new low fat sandwich!

A tent card

41.1 Make word combinations using a word or phrase from each box. One word can be used twice. Then use the word combinations to complete the sentences below. Look at A opposite to help you.

an element	coupons
money-off	offer
no	of skill
online	promotions
seasonal	purchase necessary
special	two
three for	

1 Some .... can be found on the internet. These are called
....
2 When children go back to school after the long holidays there are always
.... on pencils, paper and school bags.
3 If .... is written on the pack, you can enter the prize draw without
having to buy the product.
4 For some prize draws .... is needed to answer questions or complete a
simple task.
5 .... is a popular type of .... as you get one free
product.

41.2 Replace the underlined expressions with alternative expressions from B opposite.

These days, there are a lot of (1) shop advertising displays. As you walk down the street you
can easily see the (2) advertising in the window. These are designed to tempt you into the shop.
When you go into a supermarket, the first POP you will probably see is the (3) advertising at the
bottom of the basket. For special events, like in-store promotions, there may be (4) large printed
adverts or (5) displays at the end of the aisles. (6) Large bins for displaying the product from
which the consumer can help him / herself are often used for dry pre-packaged goods. Some
large displays are (7) put on the floor. (8) Displays put on the counter are usually smaller.
(9) Attached to the wall displays might be a better idea, if there is really no floor space for a
display. Probably the smallest displays, but often the most effective, are the (10) small static
signs on a shelf. Consumers see them as they walk down the aisles and use them to identify
special offers.

41.3 Read the remarks made by marketing managers and recommend promotional actions.
Sometimes more than one suggestion is possible. Look at A and B opposite to help you.

1

> I think we should do something with a prize. I'd like to reward our
> most loyal customers and generate some buzz around the brand.

2

> I think we need to attract new consumers and reward our existing clients. Perhaps we
> could print some pieces of paper that let people buy the product for a cheaper price.

3

> Why don't we have some little signs on the shelves or on the product itself? What about
> the ones that bounce up and down as you walk past or as you move the product?

4

> I'd like to have something big, eye-catching and functional. Maybe at the end of
> the aisles, where the customer can take the product and see the special offers.

Over to you

Look in your cupboard and find a product that has a special offer on the packaging. What
kind of POP display would work best with this promotion?

42 Direct mail and email

A The advantages of direct mail

The United States Postal Service describes the advantages of its **direct mail** service on its website:

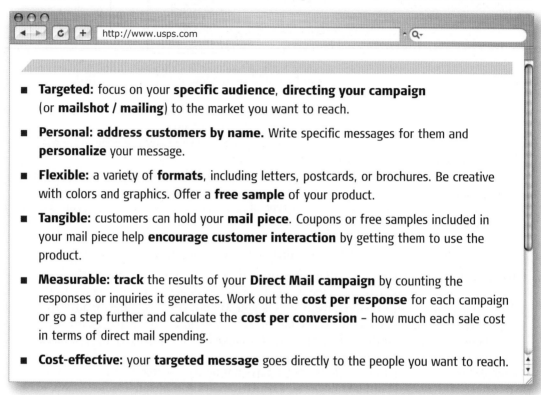

- **Targeted:** focus on your **specific audience**, **directing your campaign** (or **mailshot / mailing**) to the market you want to reach.

- **Personal: address customers by name.** Write specific messages for them and **personalize** your message.

- **Flexible:** a variety of **formats**, including letters, postcards, or brochures. Be creative with colors and graphics. Offer a **free sample** of your product.

- **Tangible:** customers can hold your **mail piece**. Coupons or free samples included in your mail piece help **encourage customer interaction** by getting them to use the product.

- **Measurable: track** the results of your **Direct Mail campaign** by counting the responses or inquiries it generates. Work out the **cost per response** for each campaign or go a step further and calculate the **cost per conversion** – how much each sale cost in terms of direct mail spending.

- **Cost-effective:** your **targeted message** goes directly to the people you want to reach.

Note: For more information on **free samples**, see Unit 43.

BrE: colour; AmE: color

B Organizing a direct mail or email campaign

Billy Yates, managing director of a direct mail company, talks about organizing a mailshot:

'Unfortunately, many first-time **mailers** overlook some of the basic "rules" of creating an effective **direct mail campaign**.

Firstly, the accuracy of your **mailing list**. You can ask a **mailing list provider** or **list broker** to sell or hire out lists of customers' names and addresses from their **database**. Work with your **list supplier** to develop an effective **prospecting list** that includes the contact details of a large number of your target audience, or people with a similar profile – the same interests or buying habits. Remember – direct mail is sent to people who are interested in it, **junk mail** is posted to people who don't want it, and **spam** is emailed to people who aren't interested. You should always include an **opt out** of receiving publicity from your company: let people tick a box to say that they don't want to hear from you.

Secondly, the appeal of your mail piece. You must encourage, or **entice, people to respond**. You can **boost response rates** by offering **free gifts** or **discounts**. Use **a call to action**: tell the reader what you want them to do. Include a **deadline**: tell the reader when he or she must answer.'

Note: For information on the Data Protection Act in the UK, see Unit 23.
For more on turning prospects into clients, see Unit 29.

C Describing a mailshot

There are many different items that can be included as part of a mailshot. See Appendix XII on page 119 for a list and illustrations.

42.1 Put the words and phrases from the box into the correct columns to make word combinations. Look at A and B opposite to help you.

| broker | junk | per conversion | piece |
| effective | mailing | per response | prospecting |

cost	mail	list
cost-effective		

42.2 Two marketers are talking about direct mail. Complete the sentences and then put them in the correct order to make a conversation. Look at A and B opposite to help you.

1 Well, if we send them a free .... , people can try the product. It's is a way to interact with the brand. We also need to include a .... to action.

2 Yes, absolutely. The message is .... and it will go straight to our specific .... And the effects are .... We can work out cost per .... and .... per conversion.

3 Perhaps, but I think the best way to boost .... rates is to offer discounts.

4 Let's get started. Can we talk about the communication plan? Do you think a direct mail .... would be cost-............................. ?

5 OK, so we've talked about costs, but I'm really more interested in your views on .... interaction.

6 How about 'Order today and receive a free gift'? Do you that would .... our customers to respond?

42.3 During a focus group on direct mail, the moderator asks questions about why people open mailshots. Match the questions (1–4) to the answers (a–g), then replace the underlined expressions with alternative expressions from B opposite and Appendix XII on page 119.

1 What makes you open direct mail?
2 What makes you reply?
3 Do you talk to your friends and family about mailshots you receive?
4 What kind of information do you expect in the covering letter?

a I only answer if there is an incentive like a <u>present for me or my children</u>.

b I give the <u>pieces of paper for saving money in the supermarket</u> to my friends, if I don't use them myself.

c Details about the product, special offers, and perhaps <u>the form for ordering the product</u>.

d I don't. All the <u>unwanted mail</u> I get goes into the recycling bin.

e I sent off a <u>card that already had a stamp on it</u> the other day. It was easy – I didn't have to look for a stamp.

f I rarely pay attention to mailshots but sometimes a <u>funny-looking or unusual envelope</u> catches my eye.

g I gave the <u>little trial pot</u> of face cream to my mother and she told all her neighbours.

Over to you

Look at some direct mail that you have received recently, and name the items sent to you in the envelope. What was the purpose of each of the items? Did the mail piece turn you into a client, or a potential client? Why / Why not?

43 Street marketing and sampling

A History of street marketing

Music bands were the first to use **street marketing** to **spread the word** – inform people – about their concerts and recordings. People pass on information by **word of mouth**, talking to their friends and family. Originally, a **street team** was a **grassroots** organization (an informal group of unpaid volunteers). The teams are not normally paid for their **grassroots promotional efforts** but are rewarded with free tickets and **merchandise** (or **swag**), such as CDs and T-shirts.

Professional street team management firms have now adopted the concept. These professional **street teamers** are often called **street marketing groups**. They can help **get the word out about** (or publicize) an upcoming event or new products and services.

B Aims of street marketing

Marketing managers choose this form of direct marketing for various reasons:

- to **build awareness**, or knowledge, of a product amongst a **specific demographic** – for example, men aged 20 to 35
- to **increase the purchase consideration** (get consumers to consider buying a product)
- to **create a buzz** so that the target start to talk about the brand (see Unit 40)
- to **establish a dialogue** with potential consumers (start talking and listening to people's opinions about the brand)
- to turn consumers into **brand ambassadors** who will relay or **pass on** the brand messages
- to **build the credibility** of a brand by convincing influential and trusted **peer members** – people of the same age or with the same interests – of the advertiser's target market to use the brand.

C Successful street marketing tactics

Street teams operate in **high traffic** areas where the target audience work or relax, such as **festivals, concerts, trade fairs** and **shopping centres**.

Street marketing uses a variety of **guerrilla**, or unconventional, marketing activities to attract the attention of their target or to **get in their faces**.

- Product **sampling** – street teamers **give out**, or **hand out**, free samples.
- Posting, or **putting up**, stickers and **posters**.
- Collateral distribution – **hand-to-hand** distribution of **flyers**, postcards, **leaflets** and **small gifts**, also called **giveaways** or **goodies**.
- **Costumed actors** and **wrapped vehicles** to create a brand experience.

A costumed actor

A giveaway

Handing out leaflets

Free samples

A wrapped vehicle

Note: Marketing can be described as **in-your-face** if it is very aggressive.
Leaflet or **flyer**? See Appendix I on page 108.

43.1 Anna Bounty works for a major record company. Complete the extract from an interview using words from the box. Look at A and C opposite to help you.

flyers	grassroots	posters	swag	word	word of mouth

Meet the woman who organizes (1) .... promotional efforts for your favorite artists.

What do you do?
I run the street team. They get the (2) .... out about events such as album releases and tour dates. I have street teamers in every city putting up (3) .... , handing out stickers and (4) .... and giving out free CDs. Street teamers also pass on information by (5) .... The fans are rewarded with free records, tickets to shows and other (6) ....

43.2 Read the information about a product launch and select the two objectives from the PowerPoint slide that best describe the campaign. Look at B opposite to help you.

Objectives
1 Establish a dialogue with potential consumers
2 Build awareness amongst seniors
3 Create a buzz about a new energy drink
4 Use celebrities to build the credibility of the brand
5 Increase purchase consideration amongst housewives under 50 years

We launched a street marketing campaign to reach the elusive youth market. The campaign targeted 18 to 25-year-old customers at home, at work and in the street. The goal was to create a fun environment where trendsetters and influencers could talk about and taste the new products. Street marketing was used to create a buzz about our new range of energy drinks. A bus, decorated in the logos and colours of the brand, travelled along the French Riviera communicating brand messages. We distributed samples in nightclubs, in fashionable bars and in stylish locations on the Bay of Angels.

43.3 Choose the correct words from the brackets to complete the sentences. Look at A, B and C opposite to help you.

1 We'll have street teams at all this summer's festivals, to help build the (credibility / dialogue) of the brand.
2 Costumed actors will be handing out free (goodies / samples) of the product.
3 We'll also be giving out (leaflets / flyers) with information about the range.
4 We'll have a (wrapped / costumed) vehicle – probably a bus – clearly visible at all the festivals.

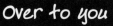
Over to you
Design a street marketing campaign for a product or service of your choice.

44

Logos

A Types of logo

The best **corporate logo design** or **company logo design** is **simple** (not complicated) and **memorable** (easy to remember). An **eye-catching**, or attractive and noticeable, image will be remembered and recognized regardless of size.

- A **descriptive** design uses an image to **depict**, or represent, the company's name or business. The Batman logo is a good example of a descriptive design.

- An **abstract** design is a **symbolic representation** and doesn't show a product or service. The Nike Swoosh is a good example.

- A **typographic** design uses the company's name or initials. This kind of design is also called a **logotype**. Good examples are the Ford Motor Company or the Golden Arches of McDonald's®.

B Logo design

A design brief for a logo might include:

Name of company	Notting Garden Supplies & Design
Company activity	Garden supplies and landscaping
Current symbol	NGS&D
Tagline / slogan	'Down to earth'
Client request	Several years ago they **adopted** a logo that isn't **bold** or **distinctive** enough. They now want something **fresh** and **sensitive** to **cultural norms** concerning gardening and leisure activities. They want to **convey** the idea that they are a relaxed and friendly company.
Client preferences: colours	Green, brown, yellow, and perhaps some red Natural colours **Multicoloured**
Client preferences: shapes	**Curved** shapes, for example circles No **straight lines** (squares, rectangles, etc.)
Main competitors	National garden centre distribution networks Homebase, B&Q Local hypermarkets
Logo usage	Stationery, shop front, shopping bags, fleet vehicles, staff uniforms

C Typeface

The **typeface** is the design of the letters used. A typeface may have a number of **fonts** with different weights and styles, such as **roman**, *italic* and **bold**. Times and Helvetica are names of popular typefaces, and Times Roman, Times Italic and Helvetica Narrow are names of some of their fonts. The font can be a **serif type** or **sans serif type**. A serif is a small line that gives a decorative finish to the main lines of a letter.

UPPER CASE
lower case

Times Roman
Times Italic
Times Bold

sans serif type
serif type

44.1 Are the logos below descriptive, abstract or typographic designs?

1

3

5

2
YAHOO!®

4

6

44.2 Replace the underlined words and expressions with alternative words and expressions from A and B opposite.

1 This logo is very <u>attractive and noticeable</u>.
2 The Yahoo! logo is <u>a logotype</u>.
3 Last year we <u>started to use</u> a new logo.
4 The logo for the Olympic Games is <u>very colourful</u>.
5 We need a new logo that is <u>easy to remember</u>.
6 Our new logo needs to be <u>different from the others</u>.
7 The Olympic logo has lots of lines that are <u>not straight</u>.
8 The Apple logo is <u>not complicated</u>.
9 We want the new logo to <u>represent</u> the company name.

44.3 Match the font types in the box with the typefaces below. Each typeface has more than one font type. Look at C opposite to help you.

bold	italic	lower case	sans serif type	serif type	upper case

1 **name of company**   *lower case, bold, sans serif type*

2 **NAME OF COMPANY**

3 *name of company*

4 ***name of company***

5 NAME OF COMPANY

6 **name of company**

Over to you

How many logos can you draw from memory? Why are they so memorable?

45

Materials and containers

A Describing packaging

At an international packaging fair, you see these products and hear these comments about what the packaging is made of and how it opens.

We manufacture **trigger spray bottles**. All our sprays are **made of plastic**.

We make **clear plastic** bottles, which are usually used for water.

Our **drinks cans** are manufactured in **aluminium**. We can personalize the **ring-pull**, or **tab**, in your brand's colours.

We manufacture the machinery that **wraps** chewing gum in **aluminium foil**. The packets are then wrapped in **cellophane**. The packet has a **tear opening**.

Our **tubes** come with **screw-top lids** or **flip-top lids**. The **flip-tops** are more and more popular.

We make **nozzles** for **aerosol cans** and trigger sprays. The aerosols are **manufactured** in aluminium.

We produce **blister packs**. For non-medical products there is usually a **card backing**. For tablets, pills and medicine there is always a **foil backing**.

We make **pots** for yoghurt and **tubs** for ice cream. The ice-cream tubs have **snap-on lids** and the yoghurt pots have **peel-back lids**, or **peelable lids**, made from foil or plastic.

We produce **cartons** in **coated paper** or **waxed paper** in a range of colours and sizes.

Cereal boxes are eco-friendly, made out of **recyclable** card that can be treated and used again, so they're better for the environment. **Sample-size packets** are also available.

We make **child-resistant packaging** for medicines and for cleaning products that might be dangerous.

You just shake the **pouch**, tear it open and pour out the food.

We specialize in glass bottles and jars. The wine bottles are **sealed with a cork**.

BrE: aluminium; AmE: aluminum

Note: A noun + noun structure is very common in package descriptions. The first noun is usually singular, even if the meaning is plural: we say *a trigger spray*, *two trigger sprays*; *a jam jar*, *two jam jars*. There is an exception: we can say *a drinks can* and *two drinks cans*. An *ice-cream tub* or a *tub of ice cream*? See Appendix I on page 108.

45.1 Complete the newspaper article. Look at A opposite to help you.

Wrapping rage

Do you remember when champagne bottles were the only difficult or dangerous packaging? A national packaging survey among the over-50s shows that nearly 70% of consumers have hurt themselves while opening a product and 75% have stopped buying products due to the packaging.

The items that caused most opening problems were ring- (1) .... cans, pills in (2) ....-resistant bottles and of course jars with screw- (3) .... lids that refuse to open. Sixty percent of the respondents said they had tried to open flip-top (4) ....

and juice (5) .... with a knife: not the safest opening option.

The products that consumers had stopped buying included trigger (6) .... and tubs with (7) ....-back lids. But more surprisingly, wine bottles with (8) .... that are difficult to remove are also being boycotted.

The (9) .... wrap on cigarette packets has inadvertently helped some people to cut down their smoking. The aluminium (10) .... inside the packet is also improving the nation's health.

And the safest, easiest packaging for the over-50s? The paper bag is still the nation's favourite.

45.2 Which cartoon best illustrates the article in 45.1 above?

1

www.cartoonstock.com

2

"I hate the amount of packaging that food comes wrapped in these days"

www.cartoonstock.com

45.3 Match the description of the packaging (1–6) with the type of product (a–f). Look at A opposite to help you.

1 a plastic trigger spray bottle
2 a plastic tube with a flip-top lid
3 a coated paper carton
4 a plastic pot with a snap-on lid and a peel-back lid
5 a blister pack with foil backing
6 an aluminium can with a nozzle

a orange juice
b aspirin
c hair spray
d window cleaner
e toothpaste
f fresh cream

Over to you

Describe the packaging of three products that you have at home.

46 Corporate communications

A The goals of corporate communications

Corporate communications aims to **maintain** and **build** the **reputation** of an organization, whether it is a company, an institution or a non-profit organization. The **director of corporate communications**, or **corporate communications officer**, defines, develops and assesses the **corporate communications strategy** with the **corporate communications team**.

The corporate communications strategy involves:

- **defining** the organization's **values and identity**. For example, Vodafone Ireland lists customer orientation and discipline as two of its values

- **identifying** and **monitoring / tracking issues** or potential problems – for example, rumours that mobile phones may cause health problems – which might hurt or **damage** the organization's **reputation** (see Unit 49)

- **communicating with the media**, with **public officials** (for example, government representatives) and with **stakeholders**. Stakeholders are people who have an interest in the company, such as shareholders, employees, suppliers and the local community. Employees are known as **internal publics**, whilst suppliers, investors and the media are examples of **external publics**.

B Corporate values and identity

The **mission statement**, or **statement of purpose and values**, is a public declaration of the way the organization conducts its business, and expresses a **commitment to** being **responsible corporate citizens** with **high standards of corporate governance** – the processes by which an organization is directed and controlled. (See Unit 5 for more on corporate social responsibility.)

C Tools of corporate communications

- **Corporate advertising** is advertising about the organization rather than its products or services.

- **Media relations** involves developing **relationships with** journalists in order to get the company's stories published or broadcast. This includes organizing **media tours** – guided visits for journalists around a factory, shop or hotel; preparing **media kits** – documents presenting information or products to journalists; and drafting **press releases** – information sent to the media to inform them of company developments. Companies often make this information available on the **media centre** of their websites (see Unit 49).

- **Financial communications** includes **investor relations** – maintaining relationships with people who have invested money in the company – and **analyst relations** – maintaining relationships with people who analyse the financial performance of the company, such as journalists or **financial analysts**.

- Companies often have an **investor relations centre** on their **corporate website**, a website designed for corporate communications and not for communication to the consumer. To **announce** an Initial Public Offering, the first time the company offers shares for sale to the public, a **roadshow** can present the company to investors and analysts.

- **Internal communications** informs **employees**, **creates understanding**, and aims to **change behaviour** within the organization (see Unit 22). Managers can act as **ambassadors** to pass on **internal messages** to their teams. Organizations have a range of channels to deliver messages, such as **in-house newsletters** (news and information for the people who work in the organization). More recently, **internal communicators** – that is, the corporate communications team – have started to exploit **social media** (web-based communications tools) to engage in a **two-way exchange** with employees. For example, internal **discussion forums** on **intranets** (internal internets).

46.1 Match the two parts of the sentences to complete the job advertisement. Look at A, B and C opposite to help you.

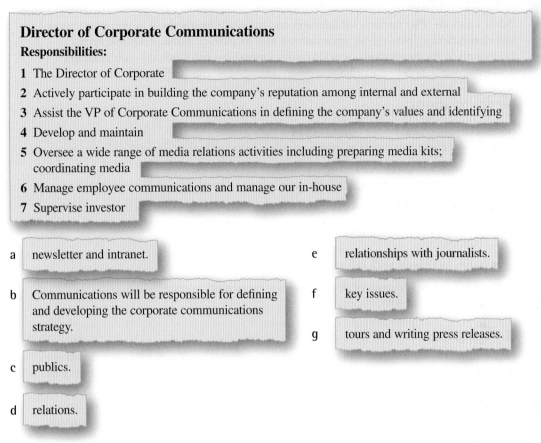

Director of Corporate Communications

Responsibilities:

1 The Director of Corporate
2 Actively participate in building the company's reputation among internal and external
3 Assist the VP of Corporate Communications in defining the company's values and identifying
4 Develop and maintain
5 Oversee a wide range of media relations activities including preparing media kits; coordinating media
6 Manage employee communications and manage our in-house
7 Supervise investor

a newsletter and intranet.

b Communications will be responsible for defining and developing the corporate communications strategy.

c publics.

d relations.

e relationships with journalists.

f key issues.

g tours and writing press releases.

46.2 Complete the web page using words from the box. Look at B and C opposite to help you.

| citizens | media | purpose | stakeholders |
| committed | press | relations | standards |

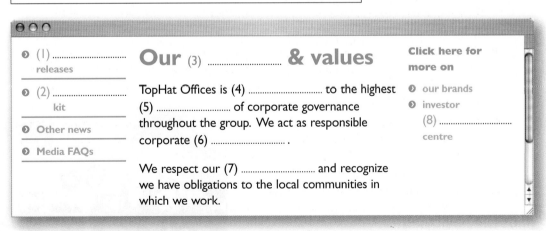

○ (1) ....
   releases

○ (2) ....
   kit

○ Other news

○ Media FAQs

Our (3) .... **& values**

TopHat Offices is (4) .... to the highest (5) .... of corporate governance throughout the group. We act as responsible corporate (6) ....

We respect our (7) .... and recognize we have obligations to the local communities in which we work.

Click here for more on

○ our brands
○ investor
   (8) ....
   centre

Over to you

Write a mission statement for a company that you would like to work for.

47 Public relations and lobbying

A Public relations

Public relations (PR) involves **establishing** and **maintaining goodwill** (a good reputation) and understanding between an organization and its publics. **Public relations firms** are experts in **media relations** (working with journalists, see B below), **public affairs** (**lobbying**, see C–E below), and advising on strategy towards public authorities.

B Media relations

Public relations firms and agencies can:

- **advise clients on** media relations, giving advice on how to build good working relationships with journalists
- provide **media training**, teaching people how to work effectively with the media
- design **media kits** to give journalists background information on the organization
- organize **press conferences** or **media briefings** to answer questions from journalists (see Unit 46)
- write **fact sheets** with information about a specific topic
- prepare **news releases** or **press releases** – written or recorded statements given to the press (see Unit 49).

C Lobbying

Lobbying is the process of seeking to **influence policy-makers**, the people who decide government legislation, and to **influence voting**. Lobbying is the business of professional **lobbyists** or **public affairs consultants** – often former ministers who have contacts with politicians. Many private sector companies, non-profit organizations or even overseas governments employ public relations firms to lobby on their behalf – that is, to **promote their interests** – to **maintain relationships with** policy-makers and to **influence the decision-making process** (how people make decisions). For example, the smoking **lobby** promotes the interests of tobacco companies.

D Inside lobbying

The American Democracy Center defines **inside lobbying** as **making a direct appeal to** legislators to support your cause. The objective is to **convince** policy-makers to speak on your behalf or to be an **advocate for** your cause – that is, a supporter of your cause. Inside lobbying tools include **influencing politicians** through **campaign contributions** (donations to political parties), supplying research and information to support your arguments, and **giving testimony** (for example, a doctor or other medical expert may give a **formal statement** about the health dangers of smoking in front of a government committee).

Critics argue that lobbying seeks to **corrupt the political process** by putting **private interests** (what's best for individuals or corporations) above the **public interest** (what's best for the general public).

E Outside lobbying

Outside lobbying aims to **influence policy** by **mobilizing public opinion** (getting the public behind a cause) or getting **activists** (members of the public or non-governmental organizations involved in political activity) to **put pressure on** legislators through **letter-writing campaigns** or **rallies**.

A rally

47.1 Complete the extracts using words from the box. One word can be used twice. Look at A and C opposite to help you.

> lobbied   lobby   lobbying   lobbyists

Labour and the nuclear (1) ....

How much influence do (2) .... on both sides of the nuclear debate actually have on government policy?

Most industries and large organizations use (3) .... , who have contacts with policy-makers.

The (4) .... industry has tried to clean up its image following a series of scandals involving government ministers and their advisers.

French energy giant EDF campaigned to change perceptions of nuclear power. It has successfully (5) .... ministers to build new plants.

47.2 Match the two parts of the sentences. Look at A and B opposite to help you.

1 Monsanto used a public relations company to promote their
2 The report confirmed that lobbying does influence the political decision-making
3 An opposition party spokesman fears that campaign
4 The oil industry is lobbying government to influence

a policy-makers concerning regulations for exploiting reserves in Antarctica.
b donations from big business influence government policy.
c interests in the EU. The firm organized a visit to the headquarters in the United States.
d process in the UK.

47.3 Choose the correct words from the brackets to complete the report from a pressure group. Look at B and E opposite to help you.

We are continuing our campaign to (1) .... (mobilize / advise / corrupt) public opinion. Following the (2) .... (fact sheet / rally / outside lobbying) in the town centre, we are organizing a further letter-writing (3) .... (conference / campaign / release) to keep up pressure on our local politicians. Our press (4) .... (release / contributions / code) generated three articles in the local newspapers. We are getting advice on media (5) .... (training / bribing / testimony) so that we will be more convincing when speaking to the press.

Over to you

A government report concluded that lobbying is part of a healthy democracy.
Do you agree? Find three reasons for or against to support your point of view.

48 Event and sports sponsorship

A Sponsorship

The website marketingprofs.com says the following about **sponsorship:**

Sponsorship is a type of **partnership**, where two or more organizations join together in a common venture. Companies sponsor all kinds of events. **Corporate sponsors** provide financial support and other resources in exchange for the right to associate their brand with the event.

★ Sponsorships provide effective **targeting**. For example, UBS Financial Services Group has **built a long-standing relationship with** the Zurich Opera House over the years. This enables UBS to reach wealthy customers and prospects.

★ Sponsorships **associate a brand with** the culture, image and attitude of an event, team or personality (often referred to as a **property**). The sponsor can **leverage**, or use to maximum advantage, the qualities and characteristics of the property.

★ Sponsorships are **interactive** – the brand and the consumer can meet. **Official sponsors** can set up **hospitality packages**. For example, sponsors of Formula One and other motor races often organize **VIP receptions** for the most important guests in the **hospitality tent**.

The success of the sponsorship depends on the strength and integrity of the sponsored organization, or **sponsee**. There are some **risk factors**, such as the potential **negative impact** on your brand. For example, **sponsoring** a football event could have a negative impact on the brand image if fans behave badly. You may need to **sever relationships** – stop your partnership – with the sponsee.

What to spend on sponsorship

Global **sponsorship spending** (or **expenditure**) is now over $20 billion. Sponsorship spending includes both buying rights (**acquiring** or **securing sponsorship rights**) and also **exploiting the rights** (getting the most out of owning the rights by developing **exploitation activities**, such as producing adverts or manufacturing gifts). Being a unique (or **exclusive**) **sponsor**, where the sponsor has the **exclusive rights**, costs more than being a **joint sponsor**, where the rights are shared with another brand.

B Types of sponsorship

Art sponsorship: some companies choose to be **patrons of the arts** and sponsor an artist or artistic event.

Educational sponsorship: a company sponsors a school, university or educational programme.

Sports sponsorship: the brand sponsors a sports team or event (see Unit 27 on merchandising). **Worldwide events**, such as the Olympic Games or the FIFA World Cup, have often been victims of **ambush marketing**, where a company that is not an official sponsor or **partner** tries to associate itself in the consumers' minds with the event. They can then give the impression of being a **worldwide partner**, without paying **sponsorship fees**.

Cause related sponsorship: this is a **sponsorship deal** between a company and a good cause or charity (see Unit 5 for more details on cause related marketing).

C Word combinations with 'sponsor'

corporate		= companies that choose to sponsor
official	sponsors	= companies that have paid to be a sponsor
unofficial		= companies that have not paid, but act like a sponsor
worldwide		= companies that are sponsors for the same event all over the world

48.1 Choose the correct words from the brackets to complete the sentences. Look at A opposite to help you.

1 Sports (sponsor / sponsorship / sponsee / sponsoring) spending is set to rise next year.
2 The England football team sold their (sponsor / sponsorship / sponsee / sponsoring) rights for the first time in 1994.
3 Today Nationwide, a British building society, is the official (sponsor / sponsorship / sponsee / sponsoring) of the English Football Association, the FA.
4 Nationwide began (sponsor / sponsorship / sponsee / sponsoring) the FA in 1999.
5 Nationwide is one of several partners (sponsor / sponsorship / sponsee / sponsoring) the England team.
6 Nationwide is a joint (sponsor / sponsorship / sponsee / sponsoring) of the England team.
7 Nationwide pays (sponsor / sponsorship / sponsee / sponsoring) fees to the FA.
8 The (sponsor / sponsorship / sponsee / sponsoring) deal includes branding on the training kits and advertising at home games.
9 In 2003 Nationwide announced it would be the exclusive (sponsor / sponsorship / sponsee / sponsoring) of women's football.
10 The Women's FA Cup, the (sponsor / sponsorship / sponsee / sponsoring), receives funding each year from Nationwide.

48.2 Complete the article using words from the box. Look at A opposite to help you.

deal	impact	leveraged	long-standing	relationships	risk

Boxfield Toys to Stop Sponsorship (1) .... **with Barbara Gasson**

As a result of comments made by Barbara Gasson, the children's illustrator, on her blog site, Boxfield Toys has severed all (2) .... with Ms Gasson. A spokesperson from the company said 'We regret having to terminate our (3) .... relationship with Ms Gasson.'

Although Boxfield has (4) .... Ms Gasson's qualities over the years, they may now be concerned about negative (5) .... on their brand. The (6) .... factors involved with Ms Gasson may be too high for this brand.

48.3 Read the texts about British companies and decide if they are examples of art sponsorship, educational sponsorship, or cause related sponsorship. Look at B opposite to help you.

1 Sainsbury's will support Red Nose Day and Sport Relief campaigns as part of a new deal. In March this year Sainsbury's sold over 4 million red noses and donated over £6.5 million to the charity.
2 In the UK Tesco is partnering I CAN, a UK charity that helps children with speech and language difficulties, to sponsor the Chatterbox Challenge. Children across the UK choose a song or story while family and friends sponsor them to perform it aloud. This year, Chatterbox Challenge raised over £150,000 for I CAN.
3 The BT Series is a unique initiative for Tate Online which lets you explore works by selected artists and ask about their work. As exclusive sponsor of Tate Online, BT provides Tate with creative design services and technical support.

Over to you

Look at the website of a large company in your country. What kind of events, charities or sports do they sponsor? What does this say about the target market?

49 Crisis communication

A What is crisis communication?

Whether a crisis is caused by a **defective product** (a product which doesn't work properly), an **Act of God** (such as a tornado or an earthquake), an **accident** (for example, a fire at a company facility) or a **scandal** (as happened to the American oil company Enron), the company must **manage the crisis**.

Beyond **tackling the problem** – that is, dealing with the problem using tactics such as a **product recall** (removing defective products from shops) – **crisis management** involves establishing effective **crisis communication**. The **crisis communication team** must **defend the company's image** against the **negative impact** of the crisis.

Most big corporations already have a **crisis communication plan** in place which identifies potential crisis situations and how to **communicate to stakeholders** during these crises. Stakeholders include **external audiences** (such as the media, local communities and government authorities) and the **internal audiences** or **publics** (for example, employees of the company).

A strategic reaction is to **go public** by communicating honestly and quickly to the general public. Refusing to comment will **encourage the spread of rumours** (where unofficial versions of the story pass from person to person) and **leaks** (unofficial information given by someone inside the organization).

A **designated spokesman** represents the company in front of the media. The organization's **public relations (PR) department, media centre** or **media desk makes official statements** (either verbally or in writing) and **monitors reactions** in the media. (See Unit 47 for more on press relations.)

Effective crisis communication can:

- **minimize the damage** caused by the crisis
- **preserve** and **protect the reputation and credibility** of the company and its brands
- **rebuild public confidence in** a company and its brands.

Note: **Crisis** is a singular noun; the plural is **crises**.
The plural of **spokesman** is **spokesmen**; **spokesperson** and **spokeswoman** are also used.

B A crisis communication case study

In 1989, Perrier was the market leader in bottled mineral water. Perrier claimed the water was naturally sparkling. The brand's image was built around the concepts of purity and quality.

A US health authority detected traces of a chemical called benzene in a shipment of Perrier water from France. Different Perrier spokesmen in the US and France **made statements to the media** before the company had **established the facts** – that is, discovered what the facts really were. These statements were later shown by the media to be false. This immediately **tarnished,** or damaged, the company's **reputation** and **credibility** – how much they could be trusted.

During the crisis it was revealed that the water was not naturally sparkling, as claimed in the advertising. The company's image was also **adversely affected** by the fact that at no time did the company **apologize** (say sorry) **to its customers,** or **express concern.** Due to the **negative fallout,** or reaction, in the media, **public confidence** in the brand was **destroyed.**

As a result, 160 million bottles of Perrier had to be **recalled.** Ultimately the incident led to the purchase of the company by Nestlé, and the arrival of competitors on the bottled water market.

49.1 Complete the sentences. Look at A opposite to help you.

1 Accidents, scandals and .... products are common causes of crises.
2 As soon as the crisis hits, activate the company's .... communication ....
3 One person should be selected as the designated .... to represent the company throughout the crisis. This person should make .... statements about the situation.
4 Make sure internal .... are informed before or at the same time as you .... public.
5 Organize .... briefings to stop the spread of ....
6 Restore consumer confidence by recalling .... products.

49.2 Label each section of the article with a heading from the box, then put the five sections in the correct order. Look at A opposite to help you.

Going public
Internal audiences
Negative fallout
Rebuilding public confidence
The crisis

1 ....
As the MD toured the country, employees were kept informed by senior managers and regular email updates from Mr Puri.

2 ....
Media coverage was immediate and very hostile, with 120 mentions on TV news.

3 ....
In 2004, the Indian Food and Drug Administration announced that worms had been found in two bars of Cadbury's Dairy Milk chocolate. Although the problem was linked to improper storage at the distributors, there was an immediate negative impact on sales and the company's reputation was tarnished.

4 ....
To minimize the damage, Cadbury set up a media desk and Bharat Puri, Cadbury's MD, went around the country making statements, meeting reporters and establishing the facts about the case.

5 ....
Within 90 days, Cadbury introduced new packaging to protect against possible infection. They engaged Indian film star Amitabh Bachchan as brand ambassador. One of the ads showed Bachchan visiting a Cadbury plant and consuming a bar of chocolate.
'Consumer confidence in the product is back,' says Sanjay Purohit, head of marketing for Cadbury India.

49.3 Make word combinations using a word or phrase from each box. Look at A and B opposite to help you.

apologize	the facts
establish	concern
express	a statement
make	to customers
minimize	the reputation
tarnish	damage

Over to you

Select a company or brand that you know well. Identify the risks for this brand. Write a short crisis communication plan.

50 Corporate blogging

A Blogging basics

Technorati.com is a real-time search engine that monitors the world of **weblogs**, the **blogosphere**. It is an enormous **blog directory** that lists blog addresses. Read these extracts from their **blogging** basics help page.

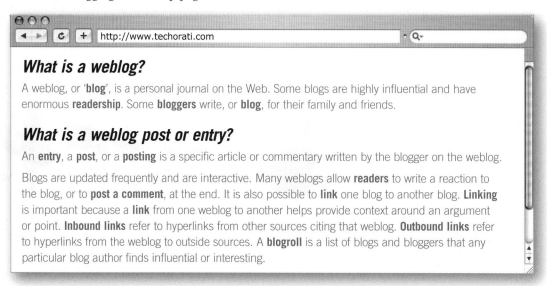

http://www.techorati.com

What is a weblog?

A weblog, or '**blog**', is a personal journal on the Web. Some blogs are highly influential and have enormous **readership**. Some **bloggers** write, or **blog**, for their family and friends.

What is a weblog post or entry?

An **entry**, a **post**, or a **posting** is a specific article or commentary written by the blogger on the weblog.

Blogs are updated frequently and are interactive. Many weblogs allow **readers** to write a reaction to the blog, or to **post a comment**, at the end. It is also possible to **link** one blog to another blog. **Linking** is important because a **link** from one weblog to another helps provide context around an argument or point. **Inbound links** refer to hyperlinks from other sources citing that weblog. **Outbound links** refer to hyperlinks from the weblog to outside sources. A **blogroll** is a list of blogs and bloggers that any particular blog author finds influential or interesting.

B Blogs as a marketing tool

Patsi Krakoff and Denise Wakeman are both experienced marketing bloggers. They advise on how to write a successful business blog on your company website, to communicate with an online audience:

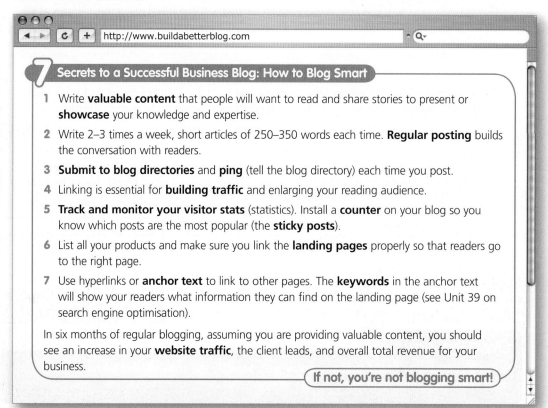

http://www.buildabetterblog.com

7 Secrets to a Successful Business Blog: How to Blog Smart

1 Write **valuable content** that people will want to read and share stories to present or **showcase** your knowledge and expertise.

2 Write 2–3 times a week, short articles of 250–350 words each time. **Regular posting** builds the conversation with readers.

3 **Submit to blog directories** and **ping** (tell the blog directory) each time you post.

4 Linking is essential for **building traffic** and enlarging your reading audience.

5 **Track and monitor your visitor stats** (statistics). Install a **counter** on your blog so you know which posts are the most popular (the **sticky posts**).

6 List all your products and make sure you link the **landing pages** properly so that readers go to the right page.

7 Use hyperlinks or **anchor text** to link to other pages. The **keywords** in the anchor text will show your readers what information they can find on the landing page (see Unit 39 on search engine optimisation).

In six months of regular blogging, assuming you are providing valuable content, you should see an increase in your **website traffic**, the client leads, and overall total revenue for your business.

If not, you're not blogging smart!

50.1 Complete the table with words from A and B opposite and related forms.

Verb	Noun for action	Noun for object	Noun for person
			blogger
	linking		
	posting		

50.2 Choose the correct words from the brackets to complete the text. Look at A opposite and 50.1 above to help you.

⬤⬤⬤

◀ ▶ C + http://www.blogorama.com   ⌄ Q⁻

Should You (1) .... (Blog / Blogging / Blogger) in Your Business?

Although (2) .... (blog / blogging / blogger) did not begin as a business activity, it did not take the business sector very long to begin using (3) .... (blogs / bloggings / bloggers) too. As a marketing professional, you may wonder if you should begin a company (4) .... (blog / blogging / blogger) or not. Here are some ideas about business (5) .... (blog / blogging / blogger) that may help you make up your mind.

• Business (6) .... (blog / blogging / blogger) is rapidly spreading throughout companies with an online presence. Every company with any Internet presence should consider the idea of starting a company (7) .... (blog / blogging / blogger).

• (8) .... (blog / blogging / blogger) may be free, but you still need an employee to write the blog. Finding the right (9) .... (blog / blogging / blogger) is often the most difficult part.

50.3 Complete the rest of the blog extract from 50.2 above. Look at A opposite to help you.

• Don't start blogging unless you are willing to be completely honest to your (1) ....

• Think carefully before you let people post (2) .... to your blog entries. Unfortunately, you may find that some readers (3) .... derogatory comments or ask difficult questions.

• Keep in mind that a blog entry doesn't have a specified length. Include (4) .... to other blogs, articles or pages in your website to illustrate a point.

• Search engines index blogs, so it will show up in search results and people will find it on their own. These (5) .... links drive traffic and brand awareness.

• Finally, if you are thinking about joining the (6) .... never forget that it is just another business tool. Plan a blog carefully and, with any luck, word will spread and you will see more traffic to your website.

Over to you

Post a reply to this comment on a marketing forum:

> I keep hearing about blogs and how good they will be for my company. Please give me some good examples of companies using blogging as a marketing tool.

Confusing words

Customer or client?

A **customer** or a **client** is a person who buys goods or a service. The term 'client' is mainly used for service industries, and implies a regular contact between the seller and the buyer. A **consumer** is a person who buys goods or services for their personal use. The term is also used to talk about someone who uses the product or service. For food, the customer is the person who buys it and the consumer is the person who eats it. However, the two terms are often used interchangeably without particular attention to the difference in meaning.

Stock or inventory?

In British and American English, **inventory** refers to the complete list of goods in stock – *We have thirty types of paper in our inventory*. However, in American English, the word also means the amount of goods in stock – *Our inventory of paper is the largest in the state*.

Salesperson or sales rep?

Job description	Title
works in a shop or store	shop assistant or sales assistant, salesperson
works for a company that sells to another company	salesperson or sales executive, working under a sales manager, who reports to the sales director
sells door-to-door or travels from company to company	sales rep (or sales representative), salesperson
sells insurance	sales agent
sells property	estate agent
sells cars	car dealer

Trade show, trade exhibition or trade fair? Seminar, conference or congress?

The terms **trade show**, **trade exhibition** and **trade fair** are interchangeable. However, **seminar**, **conference** and **congress** are not. A **seminar** is a class on a particular subject, usually given as a form of training; a **conference** is a larger event, where there are a number of talks on a particular subject; a **congress** is a large formal meeting of different groups to discuss ideas and exchange information.

Leaflet or flyer?

A **leaflet** advertises a product or a service; a **flyer** usually advertises an event.

An ice-cream tub or a tub of ice cream?

There is a difference between an **ice-cream tub** (the container itself, without the contents) and a **tub of ice cream** (the product in its container). So a **jam jar** is the container, and a **jar of jam** refers to the jam in the jar.

A jam jar

A jar of jam

Preparing a marketing plan

A marketing manager has made notes while preparing a marketing plan:

QUESTIONS TO ASK

How can I best <u>define my business</u>? What kind of company are we?

Are my objectives <u>SMART</u>? (See Unit 4)

Should I focus on <u>repeat business</u>, thereby keeping the customers we've got, or should I focus on <u>gaining new customers</u>?

Do my customers <u>share</u> any <u>patterns</u>, <u>habits</u> or repetitive behaviours? For example, do they all shop in the same kinds of shops?

Are there any <u>market segments</u> (See Unit 19) or groups of consumers that are <u>underserved</u> – not provided for enough or at all?

Is the product or service <u>viable</u>? Will it make a profit?

Is it <u>accessible</u>? Is it easy for the audience to get or start using?

How well did previous <u>marketing methods</u> work?

Which <u>marketing mediums</u>, or communication channels, are best for my audience?

Should I use a <u>cross-section of media</u> or should I just focus on one medium?

Do I have a <u>clear marketing message</u>? One that is easy for the audience to understand?

How can I ensure the same <u>look and feel</u> across all my adverts and marketing efforts?

Can I <u>time my marketing campaigns</u> to coincide with seasonal sales or product launches?

How much is the <u>cost compared to sales</u>? Are we making enough money to cover our costs?

How much is the <u>cost per customer</u>? (See Unit 24)

Do I have <u>clear objectives</u> so that I can measure the results?

How can I <u>get feedback from</u> my audience? Which kind of <u>market research</u> should I carry out? (See Unit 8–9)

Talking about numbers

Movements

Downward movement		Upward movement	
Verb	**Noun**	**Verb**	**Noun**
to fall	a fall	to rise	a rise
to go down	–	to go up	–
to decrease	a decrease	to increase	an increase
to drop	a drop		
to reduce	a reduction		

The number of satisfied consumers in 2005 was	double triple / three times quadruple / four times	that in 1995.

There was a	twofold threefold fourfold	increase in the number of intentions to buy between 1995 and 2005.

Approval ratings increased	twofold threefold fourfold	between 1995 and 2005.
Approval ratings	doubled trebled quadrupled	

Percentages, fractions and proportions

Percentage	Fraction	Proportion
twenty-five percent (25%)	**a quarter**	one **out of** four
thirty-three percent (33%)	**a third**	one out of three
fifty percent (50%)	**a half**	one out of two
sixty-six percent (66%)	**two thirds**	two out of three
seventy-five percent (75%)	**three quarters**	three out of four

Presenting a pie chart

The pie chart shows the **split** (or **breakdown**) of our annual marketing budget. We have **just over** £7.5m. Of this we will spend roughly half a million on advertising, and **approximately** £1m on promotions. We will use **almost** £3m on direct mail, and postage and handling charges will represent **exactly** 71% of that £3m. We will spend £1m on merchandising, **up on** last year's figure of £0.8m. Research, trade fairs, PR and conferences / exhibitions will **cost** £2m.

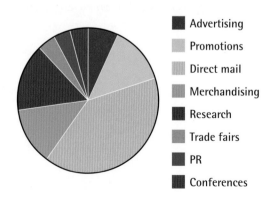

- Advertising
- Promotions
- Direct mail
- Merchandising
- Research
- Trade fairs
- PR
- Conferences

Appendix IV Describing brand values

Some common adjectives and nouns used to describe brand values are shown below. Add other words to describe brand values to the empty table. Use a dictionary to check their meanings and find related adjectives and nouns.

Adjective	Noun	Adjective	Noun
caring			
dependable	dependability		
honest	honesty		
fair	fairness		
diverse	diversity		
inclusive	inclusivity		
independent	independence		
luxury	luxury		
active	activity		
dynamic	dynamism		
vibrant	vibrancy		
inspirational	inspiration		
passionate	passion		
fun	fun		
	discovery		
pleasurable	pleasure		
modern	modernity		
innovative	innovation		
technological	technology		
classic			
	heritage		
authentic	authenticity		
original	originality		

Market segments

Socio-economic categories

Marketers use socio-economic categories to describe segments.

Social grade	Social status	Occupation of head of household or chief income earner
A	upper middle class	higher managerial, administrative or professional
B	middle class	intermediate managerial, administrative or professional
C1	lower middle class	junior managerial, administrative or professional; clerical
C2	skilled working class	skilled manual workers
D	working class	semi-skilled and unskilled manual workers
E	those at lowest level of subsistence	state pensioners or widows (no other earner); casual or lowest grade workers

Note: The **head of household** is usually the person in the household with the highest income.

Profession, lifestyle and age group

Market segments may also be divided according to professions, lifestyles or age groups. Some of these are shown below.

professional market segments	**decision makers**	people who have the power to decide what to buy in a company or family
	C-level executives	people who are high in the management structure of a company (CFO, CEO, CMO)
lifestyle market segments	**metrosexuals**	men concerned with self image and self-indulgence, living in large modern cities
	the **gay and lesbian market** the **pink market**	homosexuals
age group market segments	the **silver market**	**seniors** over 70 years old
	baby boomers	born between 1946 and 1964
	Generation X	born after baby boomers
	Generation Y	born after Generation X
	twentysomethings	twenty to twenty-nine years old
	teens	thirteen to nineteen years old
	tweens	eight to twelve years old

Indirect distribution methods

Most manufacturers use indirect distribution channels; some examples are shown below.

Distributor or distribution intermediary	Description
vending machine	Used to buy small items such as chocolate or soft drinks, by paying with coins. Vending machines can be **refrigerated** to allow for the storage of **perishable** items, such as fresh fruit and sandwiches.
franchise	The **franchisee** buys the right to sell a company's products in a particular area using the company's name. McDonald's is a good example of a franchise.
shops and **stores**	A **department store** is a large shop that is divided into different sections, such as shoes, furniture and books. Each department sells different things. A **corner shop** is usually small, **opens long hours** (sometimes 24 hours a day), and sells everyday foods and goods to the local neighbourhood. A **supermarket** is larger and sells most types of food and goods needed in the home. A **specialist shop** sells goods that are useful for people with a certain interest or need. Examples are a cycling shop or a pharmacy.

BrE: corner shop; AmE: convenience store

Note: Although **shop** and **store** mean the same and are often interchangeable, **store** is more common in American English. However, it is also used in some combinations – we don't say 'department shop' or 'convenience shop'.

Advertising techniques

Common techniques that advertisers use to appeal to consumers include:

Pester power

Pester power encourages children to ask their parents to buy a specific brand or product.

Beauty appeal or sex appeal

Beauty appeal or **sex appeal** suggests that consumers who use the product will be more attractive.

Peer approval

Peer approval associates the product with social acceptance by friends or peers.

Scientific claim or statistical claim

Scientific claim or **statistical claim** uses research or statistics to convince consumers.

Lifestyle advertising

Lifestyle advertising suggests that buying the brand will give access to an inspirational or more attractive lifestyle.

Rebel advertising

Rebel advertising goes against social norms and may appeal to teenagers.

Escape advertising

Escape advertising makes the consumer imagine he or she is living a very different life.

Celebrity endorsement

Celebrity endorsement uses a famous person, such as a footballer or film star, to recommend the product.

Puffing

Puffing uses a message that is so exaggerated that consumers will not believe it to be true – for example, 'The Ultimate Driving Machine' by BMW, or 'Get your teeth cleaner than clean'.

Dayparts and programmes

Dayparts

TV and radio dayparts and their audiences are shown below.

TV dayparts			Audience
6 am – 12 pm	morning	daytime	housewives, the unemployed, students, retired people
12 pm – 4.30 pm	afternoon		
4.30 pm – 7 pm	fringe		children, retired people
7 pm – 8 pm	prime access		wide audience, nearly everyone
8 pm – 11 pm	prime time		wide audience, nearly everyone
11 pm – 1 am	late night		young people, the unemployed

Radio dayparts		Audience
6 am – 10 am	AM drive time	workers driving to work
10 am – 3 pm	daytime	housewives, the unemployed, students, retired people
3 pm – 7 pm	PM drive time	workers driving home
7 pm – 12 am	night	young people
12 am – 6 am	overnight	young people

Types of TV programme

The news gives national and international information.

At the end of the news there is often a **weather forecast**.

A **documentary** is a factual programme on a particular subject – for example, wildlife.

A **film** may be a feature film originally made for cinema, or a **film made for TV**.

A **series** is a set of programmes on the same subject or using the same characters.

A **serial** is a story that is broadcast in several parts.

A **soap opera** is a series of programmes about the lives and problems of a particular group of characters.

Reality TV is where members of the general public are filmed in dramatic or funny situations.

A **game show** is an unscripted TV programme where ordinary people compete to win prizes.

A **variety show** consists of several short performances by different artists.

There are also **sports programmes, music programmes** and **children's programmes**.

Types of out-of-home advertising

Some common types of out-of-home advertising are shown below.

A wrapped taxi

An ad inside a bus

An ad on the rear of a bus

A bus shelter

An ad inside a train

Floor graphics

A bench

Types of magazine

Magazines can be divided into the following categories:

Category	Description of content	Example titles
glossy magazines (also known as glossies)	Printed on high quality paper, lots of photos and adverts	Elle, Red, GQ
special interest	Articles that **appeal to** a small group of people with similar interests	Inside Soap, PC Answers
current affairs and news	Articles about what is happening in the world, offering analysis	The Economist, Time Magazine
men's magazines	Articles that appeal to men	FHM (For Him Magazine), GQ
women's magazines	Articles that appeal to women	Sugar, Red, Good Housekeeping
children's magazines	Articles that appeal to children	National Geographic Kids
home and garden	Articles about home decoration and gardening	The English Garden, Elle Decoration
customer magazines	Some supermarkets produce **in-store** magazines, often **cookery magazines**, designed to sell their products.	Sainsbury's Magazine, Waitrose Food Illustrated
	Some department stores publish **lifestyle magazines** or **fashion and beauty magazines**.	Harrods' Omnia magazine
	Most airlines produce **in-flight magazines** for their passengers. They contain articles about destinations and travel tips.	High Life from British Airways
	Car manufacturers publish titles about their cars.	BMW Magazine, Volvo's LIV Magazine

A newspaper rate card

The rate card for a local British newspaper is shown below.

Position	Description	Colour	Mono (black and white)
		Price	
SCC – specified positions	Single column centimetre (SCC): the advertiser pays for the length of column needed for the ad. For example, a colour advert measuring 5 cm by two columns would cost £120. The advertiser requests a specific page in the newspaper.	£12	£8
SCC – run of paper	Single column centimetre which can be placed in any convenient place – the newspaper decides where	£9.40	£7
full page	The advert takes up an entire page.	£240	£160
DPS	Double page spread: the advert runs across two consecutive pages.	£450	£300
Special positions Pages that are popular with readers are more expensive.		Price	
centre spread	The two pages in the middle of the newspaper	£515	
front page solus	The only advert on the front page (7cm × 8cm)	£240	
back page solus	The only advert on the last page	£240	
Sunday magazine		Price	
half page	The advert takes up 50% of the page.	£330	
IFC	Inside front cover, the first left hand page of the magazine	£710	
OBC	Outside back cover, the last page of the magazine	£710	
IBC	Inside back cover, the last right hand page of the magazine	£590	
facing matter	The advert is opposite a page that contains **editorial content**, such as articles and photographs from the magazine.	£510	
half pages next to / under matter	The advert is 50% of the page and is above, below or at the side of articles.	£390	
insert	An advert is printed on a separate, smaller piece of paper and put inside the magazine.	£355	

Mailshot items

There are many items that can be included as part of a mailshot; some are shown below.

gimmicky envelope

covering letter

catalogue

product sample

promotional video

free gift

customer newsletter

coupon response device

money-off voucher

order form

reply-paid envelope

postcard

BrE: reply-paid; AmE: prepaid

Answer key

1.1
1 staff, employees (people)
2 range (product)
3 advertising (promotion)
4 accessibility, outlets, locations (place)
5 expensive, competitors, deals (price)

1.2 1 promotional   2 advertising   3 mix   4 price   5 products

1.3

Product	Price	Place	Promotion	People
branding launch quality reputation support	discounts special deals	accessibility delivery distribution location	direct marketing	competitors customers sales force

2.1
Product: acceptability, customer needs, objects
Price: affordability, cost to user, objectives
Place: accessibility, convenience, organization
Promotion: awareness, communication, operations

2.2
1 customers   3 meet   5 awareness
2 identified   4 promotional

2.3
1 socially acceptable   3 price   5 convenient
2 high quality   4 afford   6 Revenue objectives

2.4
1 We must attract attention to the product.
2 People will become aware of the brand.
3 We need to create an interest in the product.
4 We want customers to develop an interest in the product.
5 We must develop a desire to own our product.
6 People will take steps to try it.
7 We must prompt action to buy it.

3.1 1 threats   2 weaknesses   3 opportunities   4 strengths

3.2

Verb	Noun	Adjective
	opportunity	opportune
strengthen	strength	strong
threaten	threat	threatening
weaken	weakness	weak

1 threat   2 opportunities, strengths   3 weaknesses, threats   4 threats

3.3
1 The brand is very <u>strong</u>.
2 Today, <u>consumer</u> fears about health are one of the biggest threats to the processed food sector.
3 An undifferentiated offer will <u>weaken</u> the company in the short term.
4 A clear opportunity is a <u>gap</u> in the market.
5 We may be <u>threatened</u> by the emerging trend towards online shopping.
6 A <u>price war</u> has weakened our profitability.

4.1
1 market segments
2 target market
3 marketing strategy
4 marketing plan
5 marketing methods
6 marketing mix

4.2
1 USP   2 Competitor Analysis   3 Target Market

5.1
animal testing
donate money
environmental problems
environmental sustainability

mutually beneficial
responsible purchasing
social problems
socially responsible

5.2
1 partnership
2 charity
3 donate
4 donation
5 socially
6 convinced
7 social
8 friendly
9 beneficial
10 purchasing
11 sustainability

a CRM   b social marketing   c green marketing

5.3

Noun	Adjective	Adverb
en'vironment	environ'mental	environ'mentally
responsi'bility	re'sponsible	re'sponsibly
so'ciety	'social	'socially
sustaina'bility	su'stainable	su'stainably

6.1
1 macro
2 macro
3 micro
4 macro
5 micro
6 micro
7 macro

6.2
1 satisfy e
2 understand b
3 consumer d
4 relations f
5 differentiate a
6 development c

6.3
1 agreements
2 rates
3 birth
4 gender
5 religion
6 distribution
7 communication

7.1
1 registered   2 copyright   3 permission

7.2
1 Patent protection gives a company the exclusive right to market a product.
2 A granted patent must be renewed regularly.
3 Wilful trademark infringement may lead to a lawsuit.
4 Visitors to the website must read and agree to the terms and conditions.
5 Material that is subject to copyright cannot be used without permission.

7.3
1 product
2 damage
3 personal
4 standards
5 enforcement
6 entitled
7 satisfactory

a iii, b i, c ii

8.1
1 motivation + primary
2 qualitative + field
3 desktop + secondary
4 quantitative + primary

8.2 1 telephone
2 focus group, moderator
3 mail, omnibus
4 respondent, interviewer-administered
5 Mystery shopper
6 package, taste

8.3 1c, 2b, 3a, 4b, 5a

9.1 1 correct
2 Over half of their news consumption is online.
3 79% of respondents are male.
4 correct
5 The survey suggests that nearly two thirds of bloggers are over 30.

9.2 1 over   2 rose   3 significantly   4 stable   5 period   6 plummeted

10.1 product development phase
product idea
product improvement
product innovation
product modification

niche market
mass market
penetrate the market
route to market

10.2 1 limited / special
2 customer
3 new
4 technically
5 viable

10.3 1 gap
2 market
3 successful
4 penetrate
5 development
6 route

11.1 1 We should carry out some sensory research.
2 We have completed the alpha test and are now ready for beta testing.
3 The results will allow us to fine-tune our marketing plan.
4 We have planned the market rollout across Europe.
5 We have set a launch date and now need to prepare the distribution network.

1c, 2c, 3a, 4b, 5b

11.2 1 resources
2 product
3 prototype
4 flaws
5 success
6 representations
7 time
8 manage
9 forecast
10 launch
11 date

11.3 1 PS3 spent a long time in the development <u>pipeline</u>.
2 The <u>market</u> introduction stage did not go smoothly for PS3.
3 The original launch <u>date</u> for PS3 was in the spring.
4 The <u>market</u> rollout in Europe for PS3 was delayed.
5 The launch event in France was a failure because the marketing communications <u>action</u> plan was poorly prepared.
6 Sony is also launching an international e-distribution <u>network</u> to provide online content.

12.1 1 brainstorming, generate
2 criticize
3 modify
4 on, out of

12.2 1 got c, 2 back a, 3 down b, 4 on a

12.3 1e, 2d, 3f, 4a, 5c, 6b

12.4 1 ground 4 about 7 combine
2 juices 5 suggestion
3 Couldn't / Could 6 makes

13.1 1 raw materials 3 product type 5 product class
2 manufacture 4 manufacturers

13.2 1 hard goods 5 white goods
2 perishable goods / perishable products 6 brown goods
3 convenience goods 7 healthcare products
4 nondurable goods

14.1 1 The Boston Consulting Group Matrix is used as a planning tool.
2 It concerns the product life cycle.
3 A product with a high relative market share and low market growth rate is a cash cow.
4 Cash cows can be used to fund research and development for new products.
5 Stars may generate high cash flows but are not always profitable.
6 Dogs may generate negative cash flow.
7 It may be necessary to drop the line.
8 Question marks will consume resources before giving a return on investment.

14.2 1 star 2 cash cow 3 dog 4 question mark / problem child

14.3 generate profit market growth
generate cash flow market share
market growth rate

15.1 1 force 2 rep, pitch 3 agent 4 make

15.2 1 shelf space 2 a listing 3 retail buyer 4 outlets

15.3 1d, 2a, 3e, 4g, 5b, 6f, 7c

16.1

```
                    ¹B
²D I F F E R E N T I A T E
                    A
        ³O W N      ⁴P
                N   R
⁵G E N E R I C      E
                N   M
        ⁶F ⁷L A G S H I P
           E        U
        ⁸R A N G E  M
           D
        ⁹E C O N O M Y
           R
```

16.2 1 brand essence 3 brand image
2 brand promise 4 brand vision

17.1 1 brand personality 3 brand tone of voice
2 brand values 4 brand mission

17.2 1c, 2b, 3d, 4a

17.3 1 An advertising campaign is an example of brand <u>behaviour</u>.
2 The brand <u>personality</u> is a statement of the human characteristics of a brand.
3 true
4 You stretch a brand when you <u>increase the range of products in the brand</u>.
5 true
6 <u>Brand tone of voice</u>, <u>brand values</u>, <u>brand mission</u>, brand vision and brand personality are all part of the brand platform.

17.4 1 brand awareness   3 brand preference
2 brand consideration   4 brand loyalty / brand retention

18.1 1 Freshness   2 Modernity   3 Naturalness   4 Pleasure

18.2 1 flexibility   2 simplicity   3 easy to use   4 knowledgeable   5 money

18.3 1 innovative   3 Inspirational
2 Respected   4 Luxury

19.1 1b, 2c, 3a, 4a

1 Early adopters   2 silver market   3 late majority   4 customer profile

19.2 1 market   2 targeted   3 power   4 appeal   5 boomer   6 tweens

19.3 1 life cycle b   3 appeal a   5 income c
2 lifestyle d   4 affluent e

20.1 1d, 2a, 3c, 4e, 5b

20.2 1 Customers like to maintain a certain <u>lifestyle</u>.
2 A major <u>customer</u> concern is how to provide for the immediate family.
3 Buying food and drink is an example of satisfying a physiological <u>need</u>.
4 Some service sectors are highly attuned <u>to</u> customer needs.
5 The Consumer <u>Life</u> Cycle shows how consumer needs change over a period of time.

20.3 1 final purchasing decision
2 personal involvement
3 purchase intentions
4 routine purchases
5 purchasing behaviour / purchasing pattern
6 impulse purchasing

21.1 1 loyal   5 earn   9 redeem
2 repurchase   6 implement   10 redemption options
3 reward   7 Transaction records
4 loyalty   8 application form

21.2 1 card   4 special offers   7 earn
2 preferred   5 build   8 retain
3 points   6 programmes

22.1 1 build   3 turnover   5 internal
2 recognizing   4 sales   6 reaction

22.2 3, 2, 5, 6, 1, 4

a false   **b** false   **c** true

22.3 1 scheme, membership, welcome, earned
2 encourage, qualifiying
3 force

23.1 differentiate between customers   analyse data   mine data
identify customers   disclose data   process data
interact with customers   gather data   store data

23.2 1 disclose (CRM marketer)
2 stored (representative of a consumer watchdog)
3 gathers (consumer)
4 differentiate (a CRM marketer)

23.3

1 relationships	6 record	11 gathered
2 CRM	7 differentiate	12 database
3 identify	8 interacting	13 data mining
4 store	9 dialogue	
5 database	10 customization	

24.1 1d, 2e, 3a, 4c, 5b

24.2

1 Setting	5 cost	9 match
2 thumb	6 afford	10 allocate
3 task	7 respect	11 percent
4 objectives	8 cut	

ChamberE mentions both objective-and-task and affordable
MattAp mentions competitive parity
CathE mentions percentage of sales

25.1 1 captive product pricing   3 penetration pricing
2 psychological pricing   4 product bundle pricing

25.2 1d, 2c, 3b, 4e, 5a, 6g, 7f

25.3

1 unique	4 costs	7 points
2 solutions	5 sensitive	8 fair
3 significancc	6 prcmium	9 bargain

26.1

1 road haulage	4 air freight	7 a load
2 rail freight	5 delivery service	
3 container ship	6 warehouse	

26.2 Order: 6, 2, 5, 4, 3, 1

26.3 direct distribution   distribution chain
indirect distribution   distribution costs
distribution channel   distribution intermediary

1 Distribution costs   4 indirect distribution
2 distribution chain   5 distribution intermediary
3 direct distribution

27.1 1 core brand   3 gifts
  2 merchandise   4 cross-marketing

27.2 1c This on-pack offer really captures the spirit of the promoted brand.
  2a There is a small freebie inside the pack. This kind of promotional gift is ideal for children.
  3b These promotional items are an off-the-shelf solution for your corporate gifts.

27.3 1 licensing deals   3 team products
  2 commercial partners

28.1 1 public trade show   3 trade show display
  2 horizontal trade show   4 vertical trade show

28.2 allocate stand placement   increase booth traffic
  attend trade shows   participate in trade shows
  book a stand

28.3 1 trade   4 venue
  2 seminars   5 stands
  3 showcase   6 network

  a false   b true   c false

29.1

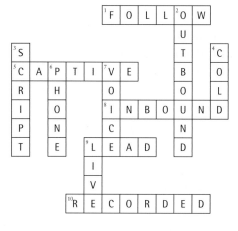

29.2 Objective
  3 Use direct marketing to increase the number of subscribers to the newspaper.

  Action plan
  1 We decided to use outbound telemarketing.
  4 We bought a qualified list from a list broker.
  5 Telemarketing operators received special training to deal with objections.
  6 We created a new script with our telemarketing firm.

  Results
  2 We met our subscription target at an acceptable cost per acquisition.

29.3 1 Hello, my name is John. I'm calling <u>on</u> behalf <u>of</u> Jupiter Software.
  2 <u>Are</u> you aware of the company at all?
  3 Are you the person <u>in charge of</u> this?
  4 <u>The reason for my call</u> is to find out if you are interested in our latest products.
  5 <u>Are you</u> / <u>Would you be</u> available for an appointment?

30.1 1 payment options   3 product categories
2 delivery costs   4 bundles of items

30.2 1 a wedding list   3 a baby registry
2 next day delivery   4 a wish list

30.3 1 Customers can <u>place</u> an order 24 hours a day.
2 No need for <u>prepaid</u> envelopes.
3 We can still have a <u>telephone hotline</u>.
4 The <u>ordering process</u> will be much quicker.
5 The <u>order</u> form must be simplified for older users.
6 Older customers may prefer using <u>mail order</u> to ordering online.

31.1

31.2   ask for referrals   place an order
close a deal   spot buying signals
make cold calls   trade concessions

1 make cold calls   2 spot buying signals   3 trade concessions

32.1 1 a Press magazines are media vehicles.
1 b Media planners work in media agencies.

2 a Ad avoiders zap during advertising breaks.
2 b Blended marketing uses TTL techniques.

3 a Normally, advertisers brief advertising agencies.
3 b Interactive TV is an emerging media.

4 a Advertising agencies develop advertising strategy.
4 b BTL campaigns don't run in mainstream media.

32.2 1 strategy   5 above-the-line   9 ATL
2 attention   6 fragmented   10 BTL
3 below-the-line   7 avoid   11 adverts
4 media   8 blended   12 tactics

32.3 1e, 2c, 3d, 4a, 5b

1 false   2 false   3 false   4 true   5 false

33.1 1 objectives   6 Core   11 objectives
2 Media   7 habits   12 reach
3 target   8 research   13 impressions
4 Demographics   9 light
5 Lifestyle   10 plan

33.2
1 patterns, strategy
2 Cost, vehicles
3 budget, mind, commercials
4 optimize
5 audit

33.3 1c, 2d, 3a, 4e, 5b

34.1 1c, 2b, 3e, 4d, 5a

34.2
1 channels
2 programmes
3 station
4 reaching
5 listeners

34.3
commercial break
commercial channel
commercial station
game show
listening habits
prime time
radio show
radio station
reality show
reality TV
remote control
soap opera
TV channel
TV show
weather forecast

35.1

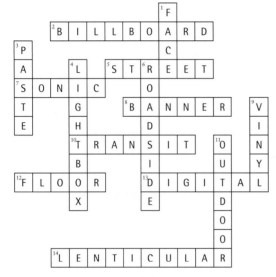

35.2
1 hung
2 wrapped
3 shelters
4 catching
5 coverage
6 graphics

36.1 1f, 2d, 3e, 4b, 5a, 6c

36.2
1 circulation figures are / readership is
2 advertising positions / advertising space
3 media pack / rate card
4 technical data / advertising rates

36.3
centre spread
facing matter
front page solus
full page
half page

37.1
1 set a deadline
2 job completion
3 graphic designer
4 printed material
5 proof OK
6 press check
7 long run

37.2 1 Marketing collateral
2 copywriting
3 print job
4 four colour / full colour / CMYK
5 final proofing, signs off the job

38.1 1 commissioned, co-produced, branded entertainment
2 branded content, mobile content, experience
3 Product placement, engage with

38.2 1 standout
2 airtime, barter
3 communication, exposure
4 generated, share, connects

39.1 paid search   search box   search engine marketing
unpaid search   search engine   search engine optimization
search listings   search engine results page
search terms

39.2 SEO = search engine optimization
SEM = search engine marketing
SERP = search engine results page

39.3 1 engine   3 listings   5 rank
2 ranking   4 SEO   6 SERP

39.4 1 rank   2 ranking   3 ranking   4 rank

40.1 chat room   social networks
general public   spread the word
live up to the hype   stealth marketing
pass along   target audience
peer to peer   word of mouth

1 word of mouth   3 lives up to the hype
2 spread the word   4 social networks

40.2 1e, 2g, 3f, 4d, 5b, 6a, 7c, 8h

41.1 an element of skill   seasonal promotions
money-off coupons   special offer
no purchase necessary   three for two
online coupons

1 money-off coupons, online coupons   4 an element of skill
2 seasonal promotions   5 Three for two, special offer
3 no purchase necessary

41.2 1 point of purchase / point of sale   6 Dump bins
2 window displays   7 floor standing
3 basket liner   8 Counter-top displays
4 banners   9 Wall-mounted
5 gondolas   10 shelf talkers

41.3 1 a prize draw
2 money-off coupons
3 shelf wobblers
4 a gondola / a dump bin

42.1

cost	mail	list
cost-effective	junk mail	list broker
cost per conversion	mail piece	mailing list
cost per response		prospecting list

42.2
1 sample, call
2 targeted, audience, measurable, response, cost
3 response
4 campaign, effective
5 customer
6 entice / encourage

Order: 4, 2, 5, 1, 6, 3

42.3
1 What makes you open direct mail?
d I don't. All the junk mail I get goes into the recycling bin.
f I rarely pay attention to mailshots but sometimes a gimmicky envelope catches my eye.

2 What makes you reply?
a I only answer if there is an incentive like a free gift.
e I sent off a reply-paid card the other day. It was easy – I didn't have to look for a stamp.

3 Do you talk to your friends and family about mailshots you receive?
b I give the money-off vouchers to my friends, if I don't use them myself.
g I gave the sample of face cream to my mother and she told all her neighbours.

4 What kind of information do you expect in the covering letter?
c Details about the product, special offers, and perhaps the order form.

43.1
1 grassroots   2 word   3 posters   4 flyers   5 word of mouth   6 swag

43.2
Objectives 1 and 3

43.3
1 credibility   2 samples   3 leaflets   4 wrapped

44.1
1 CB – typographic
2 Yahoo! – typographic
3 Olympic Games – abstract
4 Renault – abstract (and typographic)
5 Penguin – descriptive
6 Kellogg's – typographic

44.2
1 eye-catching
2 typographic
3 adopted
4 multicoloured
5 memorable
6 distinctive
7 curved
8 simple
9 depict

44.3
1 lower case, bold, sans serif type
2 upper case, bold, serif type
3 lower case, italic, sans serif type
4 lower case, bold, italic, sans serif type
5 upper case, serif type
6 lower case, bold, serif type

45.1
1 pull
2 child
3 top
4 lids
5 cartons
6 sprays
7 peel
8 corks
9 cellophane
10 foil

45.2
Cartoon 1

45.3
1d, 2e, 3a, 4f, 5b, 6c

46.1
1b, 2c, 3f, 4e, 5g, 6a, 7d

46.2
1 press
2 media
3 purpose
4 committed
5 standards
6 citizens
7 stakeholders
8 relations

47.1
1 lobby
2 lobbyists
3 lobbyists
4 lobbying
5 lobbied

47.2 1c, 2d, 3b, 4a

47.3
1 mobilize
2 rally
3 campaign
4 release
5 training

48.1
1 sponsorship
2 sponsorship
3 sponsor
4 sponsoring
5 sponsoring
6 sponsor
7 sponsorship
8 sponsorship
9 sponsor
10 sponsee

48.2
1 deal
2 relationships
3 long-standing
4 leveraged
5 impact
6 risk

48.3
1 cause related sponsorship
2 educational sponsorship / cause related sponsorship
3 art sponsorship

49.1
1 defective
2 crisis, plan
3 spokesman / spokesperson, official
4 audiences / publics, go
5 media, rumours
6 defective

49.2
3 The crisis
2 Negative fallout
4 Going public
1 Internal audiences
5 Rebuilding public confidence

49.3
apologize to customers
establish the facts
express concern
make a statement
minimize damage
tarnish the reputation

Verb	Noun for action	Noun for object	Noun for person
blog	blogging	blog	blogger
link	linking	link	
post	posting	post	

50.2
1 Blog
2 blogging
3 blogs
4 blog
5 blogging
6 blogging
7 blog
8 Blogging
9 blogger

50.3
1 readers
2 comments
3 post
4 links
5 inbound
6 blogosphere

Index

The numbers in the index are Unit numbers, not page numbers.

donation /dəˈneɪʃən/ 5
double /ˈdʌbəl/ 9
download /ˌdaʊnˈləʊd/ 7
downward trend /ˌdaʊnwəd ˈtrend/ 9
draw attention to /ˌdrɔː əˈtenʃən tuː/ 32
drinks can /drɪŋks kæn/ 45
drip strategies /ˈdrɪp ˌstrætədʒiz/ 33
drop the line /ˈdrɒp ðə ˌlaɪn/ 14
dummy /ˈdʌmi/ 37
dump bin /ˈdʌmp ˌbɪn/ 41
durable goods /ˈdjʊərəbəl ˌgʊdz/ 13
durables /ˈdjʊərəbəlz/ 13
e-coupon /ˈiː ˌkuːpɒn/ 41
e-voucher /ˈiː ˌvaʊtʃəʳ/ 21
early adopter /ˌɜːli əˈdɒptəʳ/ 19
early majority /ˌɜːli məˈdʒɒrəti/ 19
earn and burn /ˌɜːn ənd ˈbɜːn/ 21
earn points /ˌɜːn ˈpɔɪnts/ 21
ease of comparison /iːz əv kəmˈpærɪsən/ 25
easy to access /ˌiːzi tuː ˈækses/ 2
eco-friendly /ˈiːkəʊˌfrendli/ 5
economic factors /ˌiːkəˈnɒmɪk ˈfæktəz/ 6
economy brand /ɪˈkɒnəmi ˌbrænd/ 16
economy pricing /ɪˈkɒnəmi ˌpraɪsɪŋ/ 25
education /ˌedʒʊˈkeɪʃən/ 19
educational sponsorship /edʒʊˌkeɪʃənəl ˈspɒntsəʃɪp/ 48
element of skill /ˈelɪmənt əv ˈskɪl/ 41
eliminate the middleman /ɪˌlɪmɪneɪt ðə ˈmɪdəlmæn/ 26
'email this page' /ˌiːmeɪl ðɪs ˈpeɪdʒ/ 40
embed brand values /ɪmˌbed ˌbrænd ˈvæljuːz/ 38
embossing /ɪmˈbɒsɪŋ/ 37
emerging media /ɪˌmɜːdʒɪŋ ˈmiːdiə/ 32
emerging trend /ɪˌmɜːdʒɪŋ ˈtrend/ 3
employee /ɪmˈplɔɪiː/ 1, 6
encrypt information /ɪnˌkrɪpt ɪnfəˈmeɪʃən/ 23
enforce the copyright /ɪnˌfɔːs ðə ˈkɒpiraɪt/ 7
enforce the trademark /ɪnˌfɔːs ðə ˈtreɪdmɑːk/ 7
enforcement /ɪnˈfɔːsmənt/ 7
engage with consumers /ɪnˌgeɪdʒ wɪð kənˈsjuːməz/ 38
enhance a brand /ɪnˈhɑːns ə ˌbrænd/ 17
entertainment /ˌentəˈteɪnmənt/ 38
entertainment property /ˌentəˌteɪnmənt ˈprɒpəti/ 38
entice to respond /ɪnˌtaɪs tuː rɪˈspɒnd/ 42
entrant /ˈentrənt/ 41
environmental /ɪnˌvaɪərənˌmentəl/
    concerns /kənˈsɜːnz/ 5
    protection /prəˈtekʃən/ 5
    sustainability /səsteɪnəˈbɪləti/ 5
environmentally-friendly /ɪnˌvaɪərənmentəli ˈfrendli/ 5
equivalent airtime /ɪˌkwɪvələnt ˈeətaɪm/ 38
establish /ɪˌstæblɪʃ/

a brand /ə ˈbrænd/ 17
a dialogue /ə ˈdaɪəlɒg/ 43
goodwill /gʊdˈwɪl/ 47
the facts /ðə ˈfækts/ 49
established /ɪˈstæblɪʃt/ 14
esteem need /ɪˈstiːm ˌniːd/ 20
estimate /ˈestɪmət/ 37
ethical /ˈeθɪkəl/ 5
ethnicity /eθˈnɪsəti/ 19
evaluate ideas /ɪˌvæljueɪt aɪˈdɪəz/ 12
event /ɪˈvent/ 22
event profile /ɪˌvent ˈprəʊfaɪl/ 28
exclusive /ɪksˌkluːsɪv/
    right /ˈraɪt/ 7, 48
    sponsor /ˈspɒnsəʳ/ 48
    territory /ˈterɪtəri/ 31
executive summary /ɪgˌzekjətɪv ˈsʌməri/ 4
exhibitor /ɪgˈzɪbɪtəʳ/ 28
expenditure /ɪkˈspendɪtʃəʳ/ 48
exploit strengths /ekˌsplɔɪt ˈstreŋθs/ 3
exploit the rights /ekˌsplɔɪt ðə ˈraɪts/ 48
exploitation activities /eksplɔɪˈteɪʃən ækˌtɪvətiz/ 48
express concern /ɪkˌspres kənˈsɜːn/ 49
external /ɪkˌstɜːnəl/
    audiences /ˈɔːdiəntsɪz/ 49
    publics /ˈpʌblɪks/ 46
external factors /ɪkˈstɜːnəl ˌfæktəz/ 3
eye-catching /ˈaɪˌkætʃɪŋ/ 35, 44
fact sheet /ˈfækt ˌʃiːt/ 47
fair /feəʳ/ 18
fair price /ˌfeə ˈpraɪs/ 25
fall /fɔːl/ 9
fast moving consumer goods (FMCG) /ˌfɑːst ˌmuːvɪŋ kənˈsjuːmə ˌgʊdz/ 13
fast-growing /ˌfɑːst ˈgrəʊɪŋ/ 14
fatigue /fəˈtiːg/ 21
feedback /ˈfiːdbæk/ 8
feel strongly about /ˌfiːl ˈstrɒŋli əˌbaʊt/ 9
festival /ˈfestɪvəl/ 43
fickle /ˈfɪkəl/ 21
field research /ˈfiːld rɪˌsɜːtʃ/ 8
field salespeople /ˈfiːld ˌseɪlzpiːpəl/ 31
fill in /fɪl ˈɪn/ 8
final /ˈfaɪnəl/
    proofing /ˈpruːfɪŋ/ 37
    purchasing decision /ˈpɜːtʃəsɪŋ dɪˌsɪʒən/ 20
    run /ˈrʌn/ 37
financial analyst /faɪˌnænʃəl ˌænəlɪst/ 46
financial communications /faɪˌnænʃəl kəmjuːnɪˈkeɪʃənz/ 46
fine-tune /ˌfaɪn ˈtjuːn/ 11
finishing /ˈfɪnɪʃɪŋ/ 37
fix a deadline /ˌfɪks ə ˈdedlaɪn/ 37
fix a price /ˌfɪks ə ˈpraɪs/ 25
flagship brand /ˈflægʃɪp ˌbrænd/ 16
flexible /ˈfleksɪbəl/ 42
flighting patterns /ˈflaɪtɪŋ ˌpætənz/ 33
flip-top /ˈflɪp ˌtɒp/ 45
floor graphics /ˈflɔː ˌgræfɪks/ 35
floor space /ˈflɔː ˌspeɪs/ 28
floor-standing display /ˌflɔː ˌstændɪŋ dɪˈspleɪ/ 41

flyer /ˈflaɪəʳ/ 43
focus /ˈfəʊkəs/ 12
focus group /ˈfəʊkəs ˌgruːp/ 8, 10
focus on /ˈfəʊkəs ɒn/ 12
foil backing /ˈfɔɪl ˌbækɪŋ/ 45
folding /ˈfəʊldɪŋ/ 37
follow-up call /ˈfɒləʊ ʌp ˌkɔːl/ 29, 31
font /fɒnt/ 44
forecast revenues /ˌfɔːkɑːst ˈrevənjuːz/ 24
forecast sales /ˌfɔːkɑːst ˈseɪlz/ 11
formal statement /ˌfɔːməl ˈsteɪtmənt/ 47
format /ˈfɔːmæt/ 36, 42
fortnightly /ˈfɔːtnaɪtli/ 36
four As /ˌfɔːr ˈeɪz/ 2
four colour process /ˌfɔː ˌkʌlə ˈprəʊses/ 37
four Cs /ˌfɔː ˈsiːz/ 2
four Os /ˌfɔːr ˈəʊz/ 2
fragmented /frægˈmentɪd/ 32
free /ˌfriː/
    gift /ˈgɪft/ 42
    sample /ˈsɑːmpəl/ 42, 43
    to enter /tuː ˈentəʳ/ 41
    -to-air /tuː ˈeəʳ/ 34
freebie /ˈfriːbi/ 27
Freephone number /ˈfriːfəʊn ˌnʌmbəʳ/ 30
freesheet /ˈfriːʃiːt/ 36
freight /freɪt/ 26
frequency /ˈfriːkwəntsi/ 33
fresh /freʃ/ 18, 44
front office systems /ˌfrʌnt ˌɒfɪs ˈsɪstəmz/ 23
fulfil needs /fʊlˌfɪl ˈniːdz/ 20
fulfil safety regulations /fʊlˌfɪl ˈseɪfti regjəˌleɪʃənz/ 7
full /ˌfʊl/
    colour /ˈkʌləʳ/ 37
    launch /ˈlɔːnʃ/ 11
    price /ˈpraɪs/ 25
    service marketing agency /ˌsɜːvɪs ˈmɑːkɪtɪŋ ˌeɪdʒənsi/ 32
    services /ˈsɜːvɪsɪz/ 32
funding /ˈfʌndɪŋ/ 5
gap in the market /ˌgæp ɪn ðə ˈmɑːkɪt/ 3
gather data /ˌgæðə ˈdeɪtə/ 8, 23
gender roles /ˈdʒendə ˌrəʊlz/ 6
general public /ˌdʒenərəl ˈpʌblɪk/ 40
generate /ˌdʒenəreɪt/
    buzz /ˈbʌz/ 40
    cash flow /ˈkæʃ ˌfləʊ/ 14
    ideas /aɪˈdɪəz/ 12
    leads /liːdz/ 28
    profit /ˈprɒfɪt/ 14
    repeat business / rɪˌpiːt ˈbɪznɪs/ 31
generic brand /dʒəˌnerɪk ˈbrænd/ 16
generic products /dʒəˌnerɪk ˈprɒdʌkts/ 13
get /ˌget/
    a product listed /ə ˌprɒdʌkt ˈlɪstɪd/ 15
    feedback /ˈfiːdbæk/ 22
    in your face /ɪn jə ˈfeɪs/ 35, 43
    the best deal /ðə ˌbest ˈdiːl/ 15
    the creative juices flowing /ðə kriˌeɪtɪv ˈdʒuːsɪz ˌfləʊɪŋ/ 12

junk mail /'dʒʌŋk ˌmeɪl/ 42
justify a budget /ˌdʒʌstɪfaɪ ə 'bʌdʒɪt/ 24
keep track of inventory /ˌkiːp ˌtræk əv 'ɪnvəntri/ 26
key activities /ˌkiː æk'tɪvətiz/ 11
key findings /ˌkiː 'faɪndɪŋz/ 9
key to success /ˌkiː tə sək'ses/ 22
keyword /'kiːwɜːd/ 39, 50
keyword stuffing /'kiːwɜːd ˌstʌfɪŋ/ 39
lack of /læk ɒv/ 3
laggards /'lægədz/ 19
land (v) /lænd/ 26
landing pages /'lændɪŋ ˌpeɪdʒɪz/ 50
late majority /ˌleɪt mə'dʒɒrəti/ 19
latest figures /ˌleɪtɪst 'fɪgəz/ 9
launch /lɔːnʃ/ 1
launch a brand /ˌlɔːnʃ ə 'brænd/ 17
launch date /'lɔːnʃ ˌdeɪt/ 11
lawsuit /'lɔːsuːt/ 7
layout /'leɪaʊt/ 37
lead conversion /'liːd kən,vɜːʃən/ 29
lead generation /'liːd dʒenə,reɪʃən/ 29
leader /'liːdəʳ/ 12
leadership qualities /'liːdəʃɪp ˌkwɒlətiz/ 18
leaflet /'liːflət/ 43
leak (n) /liːk/ 49
learning relationship /'lɜːnɪŋ rɪˌleɪʃənʃɪp/ 23
LED screen /eli:ˌdiː 'skriːn/ 35
legally acceptable /ˌliːgəli ək'septəbəl/ 2
legally entitled to /ˌliːgəli ɪn'taɪtəld tuː/ 7
legislation /ˌledʒɪ'sleɪʃən/ 6
leisure activity /'leʒər æk,tɪvəti/ 6
lenticular poster /len'tɪkjələ ˌpəʊstəʳ/ 35
letter-writing campaign /'letə ˌraɪtɪŋ kæm,peɪn/ 47
leverage /'liːvərɪdʒ/ 48
liable for /'laɪəbəl fɔːʳ/ 7
license (v) /'laɪsəns/ 27
license a product /ˌlaɪsəns ə 'prɒdʌkt/ 10
licensing deal /'laɪsəntsɪŋ ˌdiːl/ 27
life cycle /'laɪf ˌsaɪkəl/ 19
lifestyle /'laɪfstaɪl/ 19, 33
light TV viewer /ˌlaɪt tiː'viː ˌvjuːəʳ/ 33
lightbox /'laɪtbɒks/ 35
likelihood of success /ˌlaɪklihʊd əv sək'ses/ 11
limited edition /ˌlɪmɪtɪd ɪ'dɪʃən/ 10
link /lɪŋk/ 50
list (v) /lɪst/ 39
list /'lɪst/
   broker /ˌbrəʊkəʳ/ 29, 42
   supplier /sə,plaɪəʳ/ 42
listener /'lɪsənəʳ/ 33, 34
listening figures /'lɪsənɪŋ ˌfɪgəz/ 34
listening habits /'lɪsənɪŋ ˌhæbɪts/ 34
lithographic /ˌlɪθə'græfɪk/ 37
live buzz /ˌlaɪv 'bʌz/ 40
live operator /ˌlaɪv 'ɒpəreɪtəʳ/ 29
live up to the hype /ˌlɪv ˌʌp tə ðə 'haɪp/ 40
load /ləʊd/ 26

lobby /'lɒbi/ 47
lobbyist /'lɒbiɪst/ 47
lobbysquatter /'lɒbiskwɒtəʳ/ 28
local press /ˌləʊkəl 'pres/ 36
local radio station /'ləʊkəl 'reɪdiəʊ ˌsteɪʃən/ 34
location /lə'keɪʃən/ 1
logical grouping /ˌlɒdʒɪkəl 'gruːpɪŋ/ 13
logistics /lə'dʒɪstɪks/ 26
logo usage /'ləʊgəʊ juːsɪdʒ/ 44
logotype /'lɒgətaɪp/ 44
long run /'lɒŋ ˌrʌn/ 37
Long Tail /ˌlɒŋ 'teɪl/ 32
low cost /ˌləʊ 'kɒst/ 18
low-end package /ˌləʊ ˌend 'pækɪdʒ/ 15
loyal /'lɔɪəl/ 21
loyal customer /ˌlɔɪəl 'kʌstəməʳ/ 21
loyalty /'lɔɪəlti/ 20, 21
   card /ˌkɑːd/ 21
   programme /ˌprəʊgræm/ 21
   scheme /ˌskiːm/ 21
macro /'mækrəʊ/ 6
made of plastic /ˌmeɪd əv 'plæstɪk/ 45
mail piece /'meɪl ˌpiːs/ 42
mailshot /'meɪlʃɒt/ 42
mail survey /'meɪl ˌsɜːveɪ/ 8
mailer /'meɪləʳ/ 42
mailing /'meɪlɪŋ/ 42
mailing list /'meɪlɪŋ ˌlɪst/ 42
main competitor /ˌmeɪn kəm'petɪtəʳ/ 3
main shopper /ˌmeɪn 'ʃɒpəʳ/ 19
mainstream /'meɪnstriːm/ 32
   media /ˌmiːdiə/ 34
maintain /meɪn,teɪn/
   a lifestyle /ə 'laɪfstaɪl/ 20
   a reputation /ə repjə'teɪʃən/ 5, 46
   current client perception /ˌkʌrənt ˌklaɪənt pə'sepʃən/ 28
   goodwill /gʊd'wɪl/ 47
   relationships /rɪ'leɪʃənʃɪps/ 47
major customer concern /ˌmeɪdʒə ˌkʌstəmə kən'sɜːn/ 20
make /ˌmeɪk/
   a direct appeal to /ə dɪˌrekt ə'piːl tuː/ 47
   a judgement /ə 'dʒʌdʒmənt/ 12
   a loss /ə 'lɒs/ 14
   an amendment /ən ə'mendmənt/ 37
   an effort /ən 'efət/ 2
   an official statement /ən əˌfɪʃəl 'steɪtmənt/ 49
   a reservation /ə rezə'veɪʃən/ 29
   a sale /ə 'seɪl/ 15, 31
   a sales call /ə 'seɪlz ˌkɔːl/ 31
   a sales visit /ə 'seɪlz ˌvɪzɪt/ 31
   criticisms /'krɪtɪsɪzəmz/ 12
   unauthorized use of /ʌnˌɔːθəraɪzd 'juːs ɒv/ 7
male / female split /ˌmeɪl ˌfiːmel 'splɪt/ 19
manage risk /ˌmænɪdʒ 'rɪsk/ 11
manage a crisis /ˌmænɪdʒ ə 'kraɪsɪs/ 49
manufacture /ˌmænjə'fæktʃəʳ/ 2, 13, 45
manufacturer /ˌmænjə'fæktʃərəʳ/ 13

market /ˌmɑːkɪt/
   a brand /ə 'brænd/ 1, 17
   growth rate /'grəʊθ ˌreɪt/ 14
   introduction /ɪntrə'dʌkʃən/ 11
   knowledge /'nɒlɪdʒ/ 31
   penetration /peni'treɪʃən/ 22
   research /rɪ'sɜːtʃ/ 8
   rollout /'rəʊlaʊt/ 11
   segment /'segmənt/ 4, 19
   segmentation /ˌsegmen'teɪʃən/ 19
marketing /'mɑːkɪtɪŋ/
   activity /æk,tɪvəti/ 4
   budget /ˌbʌdʒɪt/ 24
   efforts /ˌefəts/ 23
   methods /ˌmeθədz/ 4
   mix /ˌmɪks/ 1
   objectives /əb,dʒektɪvz/ 4, 24
   plan /ˌplæn/ 4
   strategy /ˌstrætədʒi/ 4
marketing /ˌmɑːkɪtɪŋ/
   actions /ˌækʃənz/ 4, 24
   collateral /kə'lætərəl/ 31, 37
   communications /kəmjuːnɪ'keɪʃənz/ 11
   metrics /'metrɪks/ 24
   partnership /'pɑːtnəʃɪp/ 5
   research /rɪ'sɜːtʃ/ 8
   services agency /'sɜːvɪsɪz ˌeɪdʒəntsi/ 32
married with kids /ˌmærid wɪð 'kɪdz/ 19
mass /ˌmæs/
   customization /kʌstəmaɪ'zeɪʃən/ 23
   market /'mɑːkɪt/ 10
   media /'miːdiə/ 32
match the investment /ˌmætʃ ði ɪn'vesmənt/ 24
maturity /mə'tjʊərəti/ 14
maximize customer loyalty /ˌmæksɪmaɪz ˌkʌstəmə 'lɔɪəlti/ 21
measurable /'meʒərəbəl/ 4, 42
media /'miːdiə/ 6, 33, 46
   agency /ˌeɪdʒənsi/ 32
   booking /ˌbʊkɪŋ/ 33
   briefing /ˌbriːfɪŋ/ 47, 49
   budget /ˌbʌdʒɪt/ 33
   buyer /ˌbaɪəʳ/ 32, 33
   centre /ˌsentəʳ/ 46, 49
   desk /ˌdesk/ 49
   mix /ˌmɪks/ 33
   kit /ˌkɪt/ 46, 47
   objectives /əb,dʒektɪvz/ 33
   owner /ˌəʊnəʳ/ 38
   pack /ˌpæk/ 36
   plan /ˌplæn/ 32, 33
   planner /ˌplænəʳ/ 32, 33
   schedule /ˌʃedjuːl/ 32, 33
   space /ˌspeɪs/ 32
   strategy /ˌstrætədʒi/ 32, 33
   tour /ˌtʊəʳ/ 46, 49
   vehicle /ˌvɪəkəl/ 32, 33
media /ˌmiːdiə/
   attention /ə'tenʃən/ 6
   audit /'ɔːdɪt/ 33
   consumption habits /kən'sʌmʃən ˌhæbɪts/ 33
   exposure /ɪk'spəʊʒəʳ/ 38
   fragmentation /frægmən'teɪʃən/ 32, 38

investment /ɪn'vesmənt/ 32
pressure /'preʃər/ 33
relations /rɪ'leɪʃənz/ 46, 47
research /rɪ'sɜːtʃ/ 33
split /'splɪt/ 33
standout /'stændaʊt/ 38
training /'treɪnɪŋ/ 47
media-saturated world
/ˌmiːdiə ˌsætʃəreɪtɪd 'wɜːld/ 33
mediate /'miːdiət/ 8
medium /'miːdiəm/ 33
meet needs /ˌmiːt 'niːdz/ 2, 31
membership card /'membəʃɪp ˌkɑːd/
22
memorable /'memərəbəl/ 44
merchandise /'mɜːtʃəndaɪs/ 27, 43
merchandising /'mɜːtʃəndaɪsɪŋ/ 27
deal /ˌdiːl/ 27
rights /ˌraɪts/ 27
mere /mɪər/ 9
metropolis /mə'trɒpəlɪs/ 19
micro environment
/'maɪkrəʊ ɪnˌvaɪrənmənt/ 6
microsite /'maɪkrəʊˌsaɪt / 39
mine data /ˌmaɪn 'deɪtə/ 8, 23
minimize /'mɪnɪmaɪz/ 10
minimize /ˌmɪnɪmaɪz/
customer defection
/ˌkʌstəmə dɪ'fekʃən/ 21
the damage /ðə 'dæmɪdʒ/ 49
weaknesses /'wiːknəsɪz/ 3
mission /'mɪʃən/ 46
statement /ˌsteɪtmənt/ 46
mobile content /ˌməʊbaɪl 'kɒntent/ 38
mobilize public opinion /ˌməʊbɪlaɪz
ˌpʌblɪk ə'pɪnjən/ 47
mock-up /'mɒkʌp/ 11, 37
moderator /'mɒdəreɪtər/ 8
modify a budget /ˌmɒdɪfaɪ ə 'bʌdʒɪt/
24
monetary significance /ˌmʌnɪtəri
sɪg'nɪfɪkəns/ 25
money-off coupon
/ˌmʌni 'ɒf ˌkuːpɒn/ 41
monitor /ˌmɒnɪtər/
issues /'ɪʃuːz/ 46
reactions /ri'ækʃənz/ 49
visitor stats /'vɪzɪtə ˌstæts/ 50
mono /'mɒnəʊ/ 37
monthly /'mʌnθli/ 36
motivated /'məʊtɪveɪtɪd/ 22
motivation /ˌməʊtɪˌveɪʃən/
marketing /'mɑːkɪtɪŋ/ 22
research /rɪ'sɜːtʃ/ 8
move through the sales process
/ˌmuːv ˌθruː ðə 'seɪlz ˌprəʊses/ 30
multi-channel marketing
/ˌmʌlti ˌtʃænəl 'mɑːkɪtɪŋ/ 32
multicoloured /ˌmʌlti'kʌləd/ 44
mutually beneficial
/ˌmjuːtʃuəli benɪ'fɪʃəl/ 5
mutually beneficial relationship
/ˌmjuːtʃuəli benɪˌfɪʃəl rɪ'leɪʃənʃɪp/
23
mystery shopping /'mɪstəri ˌʃɒpɪŋ/ 8
national advertising
/ˌnæʃənəl 'ædvətaɪzɪŋ/ 34
national daily press
/ˌnæʃənəl ˌdeɪli 'pres/ 36

nearly /'nɪəli/ 9
negative fallout /ˌnegətɪv 'fɔːlaʊt/ 49
negative impact /ˌnegətɪv 'ɪmpækt/
48, 49
negotiate /nɪ'gəʊʃieɪt/ 31
network (n) /'netwɜːk/ 40
network (v) /'netwɜːk/ 28
network of sites /ˌnetwɜːk əv 'saɪts/
35
new product development (NPD)
/ˌnjuː 'prɒdʌkt dɪˌveləpmənt/ 10
new product idea
/ˌnjuː 'prɒdʌkt aɪˌdɪə/ 10
new recipe /ˌnjuː 'resɪpi/ 10
news release /'njuːz rɪˌliːs/ 47, 49
next day delivery
/ˌnekst ˌdeɪ dɪ'lɪvəri/ 30
niche market /'niːʃ ˌmɑːkɪt/ 10
online /ˌɒn'laɪn/ 38
no brand /'nəʊ ˌbrænd/ 16
no purchase necessary
/ˌnəʊ ˌpɜːtʃəs 'nesəsəri/ 41
nominate /'nɒmɪneɪt/ 22
non-profit organization
/ˌnɒn ˌprɒfɪt ɔːgənaɪ'zeɪʃən/ 5
noncash award /ˌnɒnkæʃ ə'wɔːd/ 22
nondurable goods
/'nɒndjuərəbəl ˌgʊdz/ 13
note down /ˌnəʊt 'daʊn/ 12
nozzle /'nɒzəl/ 45
objective-and-task approach
/əbˌdʒektɪv ənd 'tɑːsk əˌprəʊtʃ/ 24
objective /əb'dʒektɪv/ 2, 4
object /'ɒbdʒekt/ 2
off-air event /ˌɒf ˌeər ɪ'vent/ 38
off-the-shelf /ˌɒf ðə'ʃelf/ 27
offer /'ɒfər/ 6, 30
official sponsor /əˌfɪʃəl 'spɒnsər/ 48
omnibus survey /'ɒmnɪbəs ˌsɜːveɪ/ 8
on budget /ˌɒn 'bʌdʒɪt/ 24
on-pack offer /ˌɒn ˌpæk 'ɒfər/ 27
one colour /ˌwʌn 'kʌlər/ 37
one-to-one marketing
/ˌwʌn tə ˌwʌn 'mɑːkɪtɪŋ/ 23
online /ˌɒnlaɪn/
ad unit /'æd ˌjuːnɪt/ 39
advertising vehicle
/'ædvətaɪzɪŋ ˌvɪəkəl/ 39
audience /'ɔːdiəns/ 39
coupon /'kuːpɒn/ 41
loyalty programme
/'lɔɪəlti ˌprəʊgræm/ 21
survey /'sɜːveɪ/ 8
open an email /ˌəʊpən ən 'iːmeɪl/ 40
operations /ˌɒpər'eɪʃənz/ 2
opinion /ə'pɪnjən/ 6, 19
opportunities /ˌɒpə'tjuːnətiz/ 3
opportunities to see (OTS)
/ˌɒpəˌtjuːnətiz tə 'siː/ 35
opt out /ˌɒpt 'aʊt/ 42
optimize plans /ˌɒptɪmaɪz 'plænz/ 33
order form /'ɔːdə ˌfɔːm/ 30, 31
order online /ˌɔːdər ɒn'laɪn/ 30
organic listing /ɔː'gænɪk ˌlɪstɪŋ/ 39
organization /ˌɔːgənaɪ'zeɪʃən/ 2
organize /'ɔːgənaɪz/ 2
organizer /'ɔːgənaɪzər/ 28
out-of-home (OOH) advertising
/ˌaʊt əv ˌhəʊm 'ædvətaɪzɪŋ/ 35

outbound link /'aʊtbaʊnd ˌlɪŋk/ 50
outbound telemarketing /ˌaʊtbaʊnd
'telɪmɑːkɪtɪŋ/ 29
outdoor advertising
/ˌaʊtdɔːr 'ædvətaɪzɪŋ/ 35
outlet /'aʊtlet/ 1
outside lobbying /ˌaʊtsaɪd 'lɒbiɪŋ/ 47
over /'əʊvər/ 9
overall demand /ˌəʊvərɔːl dɪ'mɑːnd/
10
own brand /'əʊn ˌbrænd/ 16
own-label brand /ˌəʊn 'leɪbəl ˌbrænd/
16
ownership of ideas
/ˌəʊnəʃɪp əv aɪ'dɪəz/ 12
package test /'pækɪdʒ ˌtest/ 8
paid search /ˌpeɪd 'sɜːtʃ/ 39
listings /ˌlɪstɪŋz/ 39
panel of respondents
/ˌpænəl əv rɪ'spɒndənts/ 8
participate in an event
/pɑːˌtɪsɪpeɪt ɪn ən ɪ'vent/ 28
partner /'pɑːtnər/ 21, 48
partnership /'pɑːtnəʃɪp/ 48
pass on brand messages
/ˌpɑːs ɒn 'brænd ˌmesɪdʒɪz/ 43
pass-along event /ˌpɑːs əˌlɒŋ ɪ'vent/
40
paste /peɪst/ 35
patent /'peɪtənt/ 7
patent protection
/ˌpeɪtənt prə'tekʃən/ 7
patron of the arts
/ˌpeɪtrən əv ði 'ɑːts/ 48
pay compensation
/ˌpeɪ ˌkɒmpən'seɪʃən/ 7
pay damages /ˌpeɪ 'dæmɪdʒɪz/ 7
payment information
/'peɪmənt ɪnfəˌmeɪʃən/ 30
payment options /'peɪmənt ˌɒpʃənz/
30
pedestrian panel /pɪ'destriən ˌpænəl/
35
peel-back lid /'piːl ˌbæk ˌlɪd/ 45
peelable lid /'piːləbəl ˌlɪd/ 45
peer members /'pɪə ˌmembəz/ 43
peer to peer site /ˌpɪə tə 'pɪə ˌsaɪt/ 40
penetrate the market
/ˌpenɪtreɪt ðə 'mɑːkɪt/ 10
penetration pricing
/penɪ'treɪʃən 'praɪsɪŋ/ 25
people /'piːpəl/ 1
perceive the cost /pəˌsiːv ðə 'kɒst/ 2
percent of net sales
/pəˌsent əv ˌnet 'seɪlz/ 24
percentage of sales approach
/pəˌsentɪdʒ ɒv 'seɪlz əˌprəʊtʃ/ 24
perfect binding /ˌpɜːfɪkt 'baɪndɪŋ/ 37
perforating /'pɜːfəreɪtɪŋ/ 37
perform in the marketplace
/pəˌfɔːm ɪn ðə 'mɑːkɪtpleɪs/ 11
performance against budget
/pəˌfɔːməns əˌgenst 'bʌdʒɪt/ 24
performer /pə'fɔːmər/ 40
period /'pɪəriəd/ 9
perishable goods /'perɪʃəbəl ˌgʊdz/ 13
perishable products
/'perɪʃəbəl ˌprɒdʌkts/ 13
personal /'pɜːsənəl/ 42

selling /ˌselɪŋ/ 31
personal /ˈpɜːsənəl/
    injury /ˈɪndʒəri/ 7
    involvement /ɪnˈvɒlvmənt/ 20
    sales techniques /ˈseɪlz tekˌniːks/ 31
PEST analysis /ˈpest əˌnæləsɪs/ 6
phone sales /ˈfəʊn ˌseɪlz/ 29
physical evidence /ˌfɪzɪkəl ˈevɪdəns/ 1
physical presence /ˌfɪzɪkəl ˈprezəns/ 1
physiological needs
    /ˌfɪziəˈlɒdʒɪkəl ˌniːdz/ 20
ping /pɪŋ/ 50
piracy /ˈpaɪrəsi/ 7
place /pleɪs/ 1
place an order /ˌpleɪs ən ˈɔːdəʳ/ 29,
    30, 31
planning tool /ˈplænɪŋ ˌtuːl/ 14
plummet /ˈplʌmɪt/ 9
points /pɔɪnts/ 21
points card /ˈpɔɪnts ˌkɑːd/ 21
points catalogue /ˈpɔɪnts ˌkætəlɒg/ 22
political factor /pəˈlɪtɪkəl ˌfæktəʳ/ 6
political stability /pəˌlɪtɪkəl stəˈbɪləti/
    6
pop-under /ˈpɒp ˌʌndəʳ/ 39
pop-up /ˈpɒpʌp/ 39
pose a serious threat
    /ˌpəʊz ə ˌsɪəriəs ˈθret/ 3
positioning /pəˈzɪʃənɪŋ/ 4
post (v) /pəʊst/ 7, 38
post a comment /ˌpəʊst ə ˈkɒment/ 50
post stickers /ˌpəʊst ˈstɪkəz/ 43
posting /ˈpəʊstɪŋ/ 50
pot /pɒt/ 45
potential for growth
    /pəˌtenʃəl fə ˈgrəʊθ/ 3
potentially successful product
    /pəʊˌtentʃəli səkˌsesfəl ˈprɒdʌkt/
    10
pouch /paʊtʃ/ 45
PR /ˌpiːˈɑːʳ/ 47
PR department /ˌpiːˈɑː dɪˌpɑːtmənt/
    49
praise a brand /ˌpreɪz ə ˈbrænd/ 40
premium brand /ˈpriːmiəm ˌbrænd/
    16
premium pricing /ˌpriːmiəm ˈpraɪsɪŋ/
    1, 25
prepaid envelope /ˌpriːpeɪd ˈenvələʊp/
    30
prepaid package /ˌpriːpeɪd ˈpækɪdʒ/
    15
prepress /ˈpriːˌpres/ 37
preserve the reputation
    /prɪˌzɜːv ðə repjəˈteɪʃən/ 49
press /ˈpres/ 37
    check /ˌtʃek/ 37
    conference /ˌkɒnfərəns/ 47, 49
    release /rɪˌliːs/ 40, 46, 47
price /praɪs/ 1
    list /ˌlɪst/ 31
    objectives /əbˌdʒektɪvz/ 2
    points /ˌpɔɪnts/ 25
    sensitive /ˌsensɪtɪv/ 25
    skimming /ˌskɪmɪŋ/ 25
    test /ˌtest/ 25
    war /ˌwɔːʳ/ 3
pricing considerations
    /ˈpraɪsɪŋ kənsɪdərˌeɪʃənz/ 25

primary research /ˈpraɪməri rɪˌsɜːtʃ/ 8
print /ˈprint/
    job /ˌdʒɒb/ 37
    run /ˌrʌn/ 37
    specifications /spesɪfɪˌkeɪʃənz/ 37
printed document
    /ˌprɪntɪd ˈdɒkjəmənt/ 37
printed material /ˌprɪntɪd məˈtɪəriəl/
    37
printer /ˈprɪntəʳ/ 37
privacy policy /ˈprɪvəsi ˌpɒləsi/ 23
private /ˌpraɪvɪt/
    interests /ˈɪntrəsts/ 47
    label brand /ˈleɪbəl ˌbrænd/ 16
property /ˈprɒpəti/ 7
prize draw /ˌpraɪz ˈdrɔː/ 41
problem child /ˈprɒbləm ˌtʃaɪld/ 14
problem statement
    /ˈprɒbləm ˌsteɪtmənt/ 12
process /ˈprəʊses/ 1, 23
procurement department
    /prəˈkjʊəmənt dɪˌpɑːtmənt/ 15
produce an ad /prəˌdjuːs ən ˈæd/ 34
product /ˈprɒdʌkt/ 1, 4, 15
    launch /ˌlɔːnʃ/ 14
    line /ˌlaɪn/ 13
    placement /ˌpleɪsmənt/ 38
    sample /ˌsɑːmpəl/ 31
    sampling /ˌsɑːmplɪŋ/ 43
    sheet /ˌʃiːt/ 31
    type /ˌtaɪp/ 13
product /ˈprɒdʌkt/
    benefit /ˈbenɪfɪt/ 31
    bundle pricing /ˌbʌndəl ˈpraɪsɪŋ/ 25
    class /ˈklɑːs/ 13
    development /dɪˈveləpmənt/ 12
        phase /ˌfeɪz/ 10
    feature /ˈfiːtʃəʳ/ 31
    flaw /ˈflɔː/ 11
    idea /aɪˈdɪə/ 10
    improvement /ɪmˈpruːvmənt/ 10
    innovation /ˌɪnəˈveɪʃən/ 10
    integration /ˌɪntɪˈgreɪʃən/ 38
    knowledge /ˈnɒlɪdʒ/ 31
    liability /ˌlaɪəˈbɪləti/ 7
    life cycle (PLC) /ˈlaɪf ˌsaɪkəl/ 14
    modelling /ˈmɒdəlɪŋ/ 11
    modification /ˌmɒdɪfɪˈkeɪʃən/ 10
    naming /ˈneɪmɪŋ/ 12
    optimization study
        /ˌɒptɪmaɪˈzeɪʃən ˌstʌdi/ 11
    recall /rɪˈkɔːl/ 49
    reference /ˈrefərəns/ 38
production /prəˈdʌkʃən/ 6
profitability /ˌprɒfɪtəˈbɪliti/ 14, 24
profitable /ˈprɒfɪtəbəl/ 3, 10, 14
programme /ˈprəʊgræm/ 34
project leader /ˈprɒdʒekt ˌliːdəʳ/ 11
project team /ˈprɒdʒekt ˌtiːm/ 11
projected results /prəˈdʒektɪd rɪˈzʌlts/
    24
promote interests /prəˈməʊt ˈɪntrəsts/
    47
promotion /prəˈməʊʃən/ 1
promotional /prəˌməʊʃənəl/
    item /ˈaɪtəm/ 27
    merchandise project
        /ˈmɜːtʃəndaɪs ˌprɒdʒekt/ 27
    mix /ˈmɪks/ 1

operations /ɒpərˈeɪʃənz/ 2
    tool /ˈtuːl/ 1
prompt action /ˌprɒmt ˈækʃən/ 2
proof of purchase /ˌpruːf əv ˈpɜːtʃəs/
    41
proof OK /ˌpruːf əʊˈkeɪ/ 37
proofread /ˈpruːfriːd/ 37
property /ˈprɒpəti/ 48
propose tailored solutions
    /prəˌpəʊz ˌteɪləd səˈluːʃənz/ 31
prospect (n) /ˈprɒspekt/ 31
prospect (v) /prəˈspekt/ 31
prospecting list /prəˈspektɪŋ ˌlɪst/ 42
protect /prəˈtekt/ 23
protect /prəˌtekt/
    the credibility /ðə kredəˈbɪləti/ 49
    the environment
        /ði ɪnˈvaɪrənmənt/ 5
privacy /ˈprɪvəsi/ 23
prototype /ˈprəʊtətaɪp/ 11
prove negligent /ˌpruːv ˈneglɪdʒənt/ 7
provide a service /prəˌvaɪd ə ˈsɜːvɪs/
    4, 13
psychographics /ˌsaɪkəˈgræfɪks/ 19
psychological pricing
    /ˌsaɪkəlˌɒdʒɪkəl ˈpraɪsɪŋ/ 25
public /ˌpʌblɪk/
    affairs /əˈfeəz/ 47
        consultant /kənˌsʌltənt/ 47
    interest /ˈɪntrəst/ 47
    official /əˈfɪʃəl/ 46
    relations (PR) /rɪˈleɪʃənz/ 47
        department /dɪˌpɑːtmənt/ 49
        firm /ˌfɜːm/ 47
    trade show /ˈtreɪd ʃəʊ/ 28
publics /ˈpʌblɪks/ 49
purchase consideration
    /ˈpɜːtʃəs kənsɪdəˌreɪʃən/ 43
purchase intention
    /ˈpɜːtʃəs ɪnˌtenʃən/ 20
purchaser /ˈpɜːtʃəsəʳ/ 15
purchasing /ˈpɜːtʃəsɪŋ/
    behaviour /bɪˌheɪvjəʳ/ 20
    patterns /ˌpætənz/ 20
    process /ˌprəʊses/ 30
purpose and values
    /ˌpɜːpəs ənd ˈvæljuːz/ 46
push back arguments
    /ˌpʊʃ bæk ˈɑːgjəmənts/ 15
put pressure on /ˌpʊt ˈpreʃər ɒn/ 47
put up posters /ˌpʊt ʌp ˈpəʊstəz/ 43,
    43
qualified telemarketing list
    /ˌkwɒlɪfaɪd ˈtelimɑːkɪtɪŋ ˌlɪst/ 29
qualify a lead /ˌkwɒlɪfaɪ ə ˈliːd/ 31
qualifying period
    /ˈkwɒlɪfaɪɪŋ ˌpɪəriəd/ 22
qualitative research
    /ˈkwɒlɪtətɪv rɪˌsɜːtʃ/ 8
quality /ˈkwɒləti/ 1, 12
quality brand /ˈkwɒləti ˌbrænd/ 3
quantify /ˈkwɒntɪfaɪ/ 24
quantitative research
    /ˈkwɒntɪtətɪv rɪˌsɜːtʃ/ 8
query /ˈkwɪəri/ 39
question mark /ˈkwestʃən ˌmɑːk/ 14
questionnaire /ˌkwestʃəˈneəʳ/ 8
rail freight /ˈreɪl ˌfreɪt/ 26
rally (n) /ˈræli/ 47

Acknowledgements

We could not have produced this book without the help of our colleagues and clients at Speechmark, who tested and improved the chapters. We would like to thank Graham Taylor for his very helpful contributions and advice. Our special thanks go to Nick Robinson at Cambridge University Press and to our copyeditor Lyn Strutt, for their guidance and patience. We would also like to thank Millie, Thierry and Philippe.

The authors and publishers acknowledge the following sources of copyright material and are grateful for the permissions granted. While every effort has been made, it has not always been possible to identify the sources of all the material used, or to trace all copyright holders. If any omissions are brought to our notice, we will be happy to include the appropriate acknowledgements on reprinting.

Tutor2u for the adapted text on p. 9, 'Marie Curie Cancer Care' and for the adapted text on p. 109 'Set SMART Objectives'; Tesco PLC for the text on p. 11, 'Health Care Event' and for the text on p. 103, 'I CAN'. Used by permission of Tesco PLC; Big Cat Rescue for the text on p. 16, from www.BigCatRescue.org. Used by permission; Text on p. 16 '6Degrees.ca' from www.6degrees.ca; Jacquelyn Ottman for the adapted text on p. 17, 'Case Study: Woody Pens'. Used by kind permission of J Ottman Consulting Inc; Learnmarketing.net for the text on p. 18, 'Micro Environment'; Text on p. 20, 'Intellectual Property'. Copyright © World Intellectual Property Organization (WIPO); Text on p. 20, 'What is copyright, patent, trademark' and 'Intellectual property crimes'. Crown Copyright © 2007; WWF-UK for the text and logo on p. 21, 'The Panda Symbol'. Used by kind permission of WWF-UK; Mirrorpix for the adapted text on p. 21, 'Fight for your rights when a deal goes wrong' written by Ruki Sayid, *Daily Mirror* 14 November 2005. Copyright © Mirrorpix; Blogads for the text on p. 25, 'Reader's survey'. Used by permission of Blogads.com; Adapted text on p. 27, 'Here's how I exploited a gap in the market, from the businesslink.co.uk website. Crown Copyright © 2007; Text on p. 33, 'Artificial diamonds may outsparkle genuine articles' from *The Business Report*, Johannesburg; Scottish Enterprise for the text on p. 37, from www.scottishfoodanddrink.com. Used by permission of Scottish Enterprise; British Airways for the British Airways logo on p. 38; Coca-Cola Trade Marks Counsel for the Coca-Cola logo on p. 38. Coca-Cola is a registered trade mark of the Coca-Cola Company; Soléco UK Limited for the text on p. 43, from www.florette.com. Used by permission of Soléco UK Limited; DrugStore News for the text on p. 45, 'Kids' art and crafts market growing' written by Alene Symons, November 1997 *DrugStore News*. Used by permission of DrugStore News; The Hindu Business Line for the adapted text on p, 49 'How loyal can you be?' Used by permission of The Hindu Business Line; Christian Sarker for the text on p. 52, 'Interview with Don Peppers'. Used by permission of Christian Sarker; Marketing Teacher Ltd for the text on p. 56, 'Pricing Strategies'; Brandon Martin for the text on p. 58, 'Dell'. Used by kind permission of Brandon Martin; Event Merchandising Limited for the text on p. 60, from www.eventmerchandising.com; The Wine Institute of California for the text and logo on p. 63; Mastercard for the MASTERCARD trademark on p. 67. © 2007 MasterCard. MasterCard and the MasterCard Brand Mark are registered trademarks of MasterCard International Incorporated; Visa International Services Association for the Visa logo on p. 67. The Visa logo and marks are the property of Visa International Service Association. Visa Europe enables thousands of competing member banks to meet the needs of tens of millions of European businesses and more than 300 million European citizens. To find out more, please visit www.visaeurope.com; MBA Publishing Limited for the text on p. 71 'Ford Promotion' from www.thetimes100.co.uk. Used by permission of MBA Publishing Limited; ITV Productions Limited for the text on p. 75. Copyright © ITV Productions Limited 2007; GCap Media PLC for the text on p. 75 'Classic FM'. Used by permission of GCap Media PLC; HOA Creative Communications Ltd for the text on p. 81 'Hotel Group Queen's Moat House Hotels UK'; USPS for the text on p. 90, 'Benefits of direct mail' © 2007 United States Postal Service. All Rights Reserved. Used with Permission; Ford Motor Company for the logo on p. 94; McDonald's for the Golden Arches ® logo on p. 94; Groupement Carte Bleue for the logo on p. 95; Yahoo! Inc for the logo on p. 95; The

International Olympic Committee for the logo on p. 95; Renault UK Limited for the logo on p. 95; Penguin Books Limited for the logo on p. 95. Reproduced by kind permission of Penguin Books Limited as the registered trademark owner; Kellogg's ® for the logo on p. 95. Copyright © 2007 Kellogg Company. All rights reserved; MarketingProfs.com for the text on p. 102, 'Sponsorship'. Copyright © 2007 marketingprofs.com. Reprinted with special permission; Tate Enterprises Ltd for the text on p. 103, 'BT Series'. Used by kind permission of Tate Enterprises Ltd; R2a for the adapted text on p. 104 'Crisis communication case study'. Used by permission of R2a; Technorati for the text on p. 106 from www.technorati.com; Mpelembe Network, Patsi Krakoff and Denise Wakeman for the text on p. 106 from www.buildabetterblog.com. Used with permission; Blogarama for the text on p. 107 from www.blogarama.com. Used by permission of Blogarama – the Blog Directory.

The publishers are grateful to the following for permission to reproduce copyright photographs and material:

Key: l = left, c = centre, r = right, t = top, b = bottom

Gecko Head Gear for p. 27; BMW AG for p. 28; Cadbury Trebor Bassett for p. 38(b); Jason Alden/newscast for p. 48; Don Peppers and Martha Rogers, Ph.D for p. 52. Don Peppers and Martha Rogers are the co-founders of Peppers & Rogers Group, www.peppersandrogers.com, as well as acclaimed authors of a series of best-selling business books; Picture History for p. 54; Stick Tea, Fausto Lovello, Alessandria – ITALY, www.sticktea.com, info@sticktea.com for p. 56; Stobart Group Ltd for p. 59(tl); Freightliner Ltd for p. 59(bl); ©Schenker AG for p. 59(tcl). All rights reserved; ©Bax Global for p. 59(bc); Deutsche Post AG for p. 59(tcr); VIEW Pictures Ltd/ Alamy for p. 59(br); Janusz Wrobel/Alamy for p. 59(tr); ©2007 HIT entertainment Limited and Keith Chapman for p. 61(t). All rights reserved; Mehdi Chebil/Alamy for p. 62; imagebroker/ Alamy for p. 76; JCDecaux for p. 77; Copyright: The Times/NI Syndication for p. 78; Image courtesy of ©DAPY www.dapyparis.com for p. 81(l,c); Royal Mail for p. 81(r); ©BMW for p. 83: Luke Beresford/CommentUK for p. 86; Sony Consumer Electronics for p. 87; Neil Setchfield/Alamy for p. 92(l); Cate Farrall for p. 92(lc); Janine Wiedel Photolibrary/Alamy for p. 92(c); Jeff Greenberg/Alamy for p. 92(cr); Ros Drinkwater/Alamy for p. 92(r); www. CartoonStock.com for p. 97; Andrew Wiard/Alamy for p. 100; David Hansford/Alamy for p. 104; Cadbury India Ltd for p. 105; Helene Rogers/Alamy for p. 108; Mode Images Limited/ Alamy for p. 108(r); Bob Johns/expresspictures.co.uk/Alamy for p. 113(t); McDonald's Corporation for p. 113(tc); ©John Lewis for p. 113(c); Janine Wiedel Photolibrary/Alamy for p. 113(bcr); Sainsbury's for p. 113(br); Chris Howes/Wild Places Photography/Alamy for p. 113(bl); Arco Images/Alamy for p. 116(tl); Titan Outdoor for p. 116(tr, c); Tony McAleer, Bench-Ad.com for p. 116(bc); Richard Levine/Alamy for p. 116(bl); Michael Booth/Alamy for p. 116(br); Transtock Inc./Alamy for p. 116(cr); ELLE magazine for p. 117(tl); ©2007 Future Publishing Ltd for p. 117(tcl); Inside Soap for p. 117(tc); FHM UK for p. 117(tcr); Red for p. 117(tr); Sugar for p. 117(bl); ©National Geographic Society for p. 117(bcl). NATIONAL GEOGRAPHIC KIDS and Yellow Border: Registered Trademarks ® Marcas Registradas; ELLE Decoration for p. 117(bc); Waitrose Food Illustrated/Jonathan Gregson for p. 117(bcr); Photography by FredriksonStallard for p. 117(br). LIV is published on behalf of Volvo Car Corporation by Redwood, 7 St Martin's Place, London WC2N 4HA, UK. Copyright Redwood Publishing Limited, 2007. All rights reserved.

Picture research by Veena Holkar.

Illustrations by Mark Duffin pp. 119; Kamae pp. 18, 23, 24, 25, 33, 34, 61, 67, 74, 88, 94, 96, 110, ; Frederique Vayssieres pp. 15, 69.